M

CW00431092

WRITING AND POETRY

TOOLKIT

Dedication

To the Whitefield Institute and Oliver Barclay for their support and encouragement without which this book would not have been written.

WRITING AND POETRY

TOOLKIT

Margaret Cooling

BRITISH AND FOREIGN BIBLE SOCIETY
Stonehill Green, Westlea, SWINDON SN5 7DG

© Margaret Cooling 1996

First published 1996

All rights reserved. No part of this publication may be reproduced, stored in a retrieval system, or transmitted, in any form or by any means, electronic, mechanical, photocopying (except as specified on page 4), recording or otherwise without the prior permission of The British and Foreign Bible Society. The right of Margaret Cooling to be identified as the author of this work has been asserted by her in accordance with the Copyright, Designs and Patents Act 1988.

Unless otherwise stated, quotations from the Bible are from the Good News Bible, published by the Bible Societies/HarperCollins Publications Ltd UK © American Bible Society, New York 1966, 1971, 1976 and 1992.

A catalogue record for this book is available from the British Library ISBN 0564 088358

Printed in Great Britain by Ebenezer Baylis Ltd.

Cover design by Jane Taylor

Bible Societies exist to provide resources for Bible distribution and use. The British and Foreign Bible Society (BFBS) is a member of the United Bible Societies, an international partnership working in over 180 countries. Their common aim is to reach all people with the Bible, or some part of it, in a language they can understand and at a price they can afford. Parts of the Bible have now been translated into over 2000 languages. Bible Societies aim to help every church at every point where it uses the Bible. You are invited to share in this work by your prayers and gifts. The Bible Society in your country will be very happy to provide details of its activity.

CONTENTS

II Poetry

Introduction

Detailed activities

ACKNOWLEDGEMENTS

I would like to express my thanks to the following people for their help in the writing of this book: Diane and Robin Walker, Deborah Helme, Ruth Cooper, Helen Thacker, Robert and Trevor Cooling. Ultimate responsibility for any errors is however mine alone. I would also like to thank Philip King and Colin Humphreys for contributing the Music section of *Art and Music Toolkit*.

My thanks to the following schools for their help in trialling material in these books:

Abbey Grange Church of England School, Leeds, West Yorkshire

Albany Junior School, Stapleford, Nottinghamshire

Belvoir High School, Nottingham

Bishop Ramsey Church of England School, Ruislip, Hillingdon, London

Bramcote Hills Primary School, Nottingham

Breadsall Hilltop Junior School, Derby

Brambletye Middle School, Redhill, Surrey

Brennands Endowed Primary School, Slaidburn, Clitheroe, Lancashire

Binscombe Middle School, Farncombe, Godalming, Surrey

Bishop John Robinson Primary School, Thamesmead, London

Coton Green Primary School, Tamworth, Staffordshire

Dovelands Junior School, Leicester

Fairfield Primary School, Stapleford, Nottinghamshire

George Spencer School, Stapleford, Nottinghamshire

Ifield Middle School, Crawley, West Sussex

Imberhorne School, East Grinstead, West Sussex

Kingswood (Wotton) County Primary School, Kingswood, Gloucestershire

Lowe's Wong Junior School, Southwell, Nottinghamshire

Lantern Lane Primary School, East Leake, Loughborough

Ladderbanks Middle School, Shipley, West Yorkshire

Myrtle Springs School, Sheffield

Newcastle-Under-Lyme School, Newcastle-Under-Lyme, Staffordshire

Nottingham High School for Girls, Nottinghamshire

Queen Elizabeth High School, Bromyard, Herefordshire

Robert Shaw Primary School, Aspley, Nottinghamshire

Rainey Endowed School, Magherafelt, Northern Ireland

St John's Church of England Primary School, Stapleford, Nottinghamshire

St Thomas à Becket High School, Sandal, Wakefield

St Peter's Church of England School, Cannock, Staffordshire

Sneinton Church of England Primary School, Sneinton, Nottinghamshire

Stevenson Junior School, Stapleford, Nottinghamshire

The Park School, Yeovil, Somerset

Ringwood School, Ringwood, Hampshire

These books have been produced under the auspices of the Stapleford Project. The Stapleford Project is a curriculum development initiative based at Stapleford House Education Centre. The project aims to produce materials and offer in-service training to resource the teaching of Christianity in schools. Stapleford House Education Centre is the national conference and study centre of the Association of Christian Teachers. Full details of courses and publications are available from: Stapleford House Education Centre, Wesley Place, Stapleford, Nottingham, NG9 8DP.

CREDITS

Every attempt has been made to trace and correctly attribute the sources of material within this book. Bible Society would gratefully receive any corrections for inclusion in future reprints.

INTRODUCTION TO THE TOOLKIT

GENERAL INTRODUCTION

This series of three books is designed for teachers who want ready access to a wide range of teaching activities for exploring the Bible in the classroom. Each book covers two subject areas and has been written with the non-specialist in mind. The activities are appropriate for both primary and secondary schools and they have been designed for use with the 7–14 age group. However, many of them are "ageless" and can be used with a much wider age range.

The three books cover the following six areas.

Writing } Book 1   Story } Book 2   Art } Book 3
Poetry   Drama   Music

These books concentrate on method; they do not constitute a systematic curriculum. The stories used to illustrate each activity are meant only as examples. Teachers are encouraged to apply these activities to the biblical material within their own syllabuses. They should not feel that the application of the activities is restricted to the biblical examples given in these books.

Biblical stories

Usually between two and four Bible stories are given to illustrate each activity. They are the type of material on which the activity in question works well. Full textual references are given, but teachers are not expected to use all of these. For example, if a story appears in all four Gospels, all four references are usually given so that the teacher can choose which account they prefer. The references are based on the Good News version unless indicated otherwise.

Teachers may not wish to use all of a biblical story suggested – some contain parts which are unsuitable for young children: for example with younger children the story of Jericho is best ended before the massacre. Biblical stories are often better retold by the teacher or read from a modern retelling of the stories rather than directly from the text. Information on relevant books can be found on page 23, *Story and Drama Toolkit*.

Health and safety

As with any subject, all activities and materials used in RE should be safe, this particularly applies to art materials.

Examples of pupil work

Pupil work has been included where appropriate. Different numbering systems for year groups are used in various parts of the British Isles. Most of the pupil work in this book comes from England and Northern Ireland where the following numbering systems are used.

England
Year 3 (7–8), Year 4 (8–9), Year 5 (9–10), Year 6 (10–11), Year 7 (11–12), Year 8 (12–13), Year 9 (13–14).

Northern Ireland
P4 (7–8), P5 (8–9), P6 (9–10), P7 (10–11), Year 1 (11–12), Year 2 (12–13), Year 3 (13–14).

Pupil work representing a full ability range has been used. It can be depressing for teachers to see only work by the most able pupils! The pupil work in this book is not always accurate, as it has been created by pupils with a wide age and ability range. Such inaccuracies have been retained for the sake of authenticity.

Abbreviations used

Unless otherwise stated, biblical quotations are from the Good News Bible. Otherwise the following abbreviations are used to indicate the version of the Bible being quoted.

AV   Authorized Version
RSV   Revised Standard Version
NIV   New International Version

Photocopying

The material in this book is not photocopiable unless specifically indicated on the relevant page. Photocopies may only be made for use within the purchasing institution.

USING THE TOOLKIT

Subject areas

Each book in this series covers two subject areas: for example, story and drama. Each area is presented in two chapters, the first introducing the subject area and the second detailing activities.

The first, introductory chapter will contain at least the following four sections.

1. Background. A brief introduction to how the subject area can be used to explore the Bible.

2. Resource List. A list of general resources on the subject area.

3. The place of the subject area in the Bible. A brief exploration of the place of the subject area in the Bible, for example, drama in the Bible.

4. Numbered activities. These sections bear headings such as "Thirty art activities" and present brief descriptions of activities for the classroom which are not elaborated in detail.

The second chapter contains a number of detailed descriptions of activities showing how they can be applied to example Bible stories.

Each section detailing an activity is laid out as follows.

- Bible stories with references
- Description of the activity
- Examples of pupil work (where applicable)
- Biblical application

Selecting appropriate activities

Teachers can select in two ways.

Either: Look up the story you wish to teach in the story index at the back of the book and select from the activities which use that story as an example. So, if you wish to teach the story of the Prodigal Son, you will find activities using this story on pages 31, 39, 55, *Writing and Poetry Toolkit.*

Or: Decide on the subject area you would like to use. For example, you might decide you want to teach the parable of the Prodigal Son and you would like to use a writing activity. Look through the writing activities and select any activity you think suits the story, the time you have available, and the pupils you teach. It does not matter if the story you wish to tell does not occur in the examples. For example, to teach the Prodigal Son you might select "Letters and Postcards" on page 39, *Writing and Poetry Toolkit.*

IMPORTANT NOTE: Classifying activities is difficult, for some work equally well as poetry, writing, or drama. Many poetry activities work well as prose and vice versa. Story activities such as "Conversations" also work well as drama. Teachers are advised, therefore, not to restrict themselves to one area, as there may be appropriate activities which can be adapted from other subject areas.

USING THE EXPRESSIVE ARTS IN RE

The expressive arts have a long association with the Christian faith and still play an important part in Christian life and worship. Despite the occasional period of iconoclasm, Christians have used the arts as a means of expressing faith and worship in forms as diverse as icon, church architecture, and the novel. The writers of the Bible themselves utilized the expressive arts in, for example, poetry, story, song, the drama of ritual and prophetic action.

In the classroom the role of the arts is not just to decorate pieces of work or enliven lessons, but to encourage pupils to explore Christianity and express their own ideas. Of course, the arts may enliven a lesson or decorate a piece of work, but that is not their prime function.

Content and meaning

The focus of the majority of activities in these books is the exploration of the meaning and significance of biblical material. A smaller number of the activities are designed for mastering its content. However, content and meaning should not be considered to be mutually exclusive: content has to be mastered in order that significance can be explored in depth. Expression without research, creativity without content can lead to superficial work: both are needed for successful learning.

Skills versus expression

The teaching of specific skills, such as poetry activities, may be seen as an unnecessary curtailing of the pupils' freedom to express themselves. However, this should not be seen as an "either–or" choice. The skills are essential as they are the means by which the pupils are freed to express themselves. Some techniques, by restricting a child to a specific range of tasks, actually enable the pupil to explore the subject matter in a depth they would be unlikely to achieve if left to their own devices. For example, the restriction to a set number of syllables in Haiku writing forces the pupil to choose words very carefully.

Active and passive learning

In discussion of teaching methods the following is often considered to be true:

Good = active = informal

Bad = passive = formal

Such categories are too simplistic. A good learning activity is one which engages pupils so that they become involved with the subject matter. A poor learning activity is one which fails to engage them.

If we wish to describe good learning activities as "active" ones, it must be remembered that "active" need not necessarily mean physically active. The key characteristic of successful active learning is that the pupil is engaged by the content. For example, it is quite possible for pupils to be physically active in a drama "acting out" a story but never engage with it. On the other hand pupils can listen to a well-told story without being physically active whilst being totally engaged at the level of mind and emotion.

Good teaching can be formal and physically passive as long as it stimulates pupils to reprocess the information and use the insights they have acquired, expressing them in their own way.

Conversation

A lot of good RE happens in conversation and time for talk needs to be built into activities. Many of the activities in these books will only work at a shallow level, if pupils are not given time to discuss the ideas involved with either their peers or their teacher. The classroom may be the only place in which pupils are able to discuss religious issues. Many inhabit an otherwise secular world in which talk of God would be a conversation stopper.

Many of the activities in this book act as conversation starters. For example, during trialling, the senses activity on page 105 of *Writing and Poetry Toolkit* led to a surprisingly profound conversation on the nature of God.

The limits of the arts in RE

There should be limits to the use of the arts in RE, not because they do not work but because they can be too effective! It is important to be sensitive, and some activities ought not to be used with certain material. For example, it would be quite inappropriate to enter into a graphic retelling of the crucifixion story which focused on the horrors of this method of execution.

There are times when methods which provide more distance from the material are needed, for example using puppets, video, "formal" writing activities, rather than the "involvement in" type of activity.

Respecting pupil integrity

When exploring a biblical story, it is important to be sensitive towards the pupils' own beliefs (or lack of them) and the faith commitment of their families. The most effective way of achieving this is to use what is called "owning and grounding" language. This means that we always speak of a particular Bible story as belonging to the Christian religion. For example, stories can be introduced with statements such as, "Today we are going to look at a story which is very important to Christians". Christian beliefs should be prefaced with a phrase such as "Christians believe" rather than inclusive language such as "We all ..." or "You should ...". This allows pupils the freedom to identify with the story if they are Christians, or to explore it from another standpoint if they are not.

I have retained the terms BC, AD and Old Testament as these are the terms used by the Christian community and this is a book about the Christian Bible. Teachers may wish to change these terms to BCE, CE and Hebrew Bible.

CONCEPT CRACKING

This is a planning process developed by the Stapleford Project which aims to bring out the central ideas contained in a Bible story or belief. Those ideas can then be explored using the arts. The process can be broken down into four main stages using the mnemonic U-S-E-R. It can be used to develop a structure for one lesson or activity, or for a series of lessons, or a unit of work. By emphasizing one main route through a story, theme or festival, it allows you to revisit stories and emphasize other aspects at another date.

Concept cracking an idea: forgiveness

Stage 1: Unpack the idea

Example: What is forgiveness really about? Forgiveness is about being sorry; it is about changing for the better when you have been forgiven. It is not exacting revenge when you have a right to "get your own back".

Stage 2: Select one main idea from the many ideas to follow up

Example: Changing for the better after being forgiven.

Stage 3: Engage with the pupils' experience

Example: This can be done by directly drawing on the pupils' experience or in other ways, such as through fiction – for example, the story of how Eustace changed in *The Voyage of the Dawn Treader* by C S Lewis.

Stage 4: Religious and Relevant

Introduce the religious material and make it relevant.

Example: Tell one or more stories of forgiveness and change such as Zacchaeus (Luke 19.1–10) and Jesus' story of the Two Debtors (Luke 7.36–50). (See pages 27–30, *Story and Drama* for more). Explore these stories with the pupils using activities such as "Snatches" on page 34, *Writing and Poetry* and "What are stories for?" page 38, *Story and Drama*.

Relevance

Show the story's relevance for modern Christians today. Tell a modern story of a person who was forgiven and who showed by the way they behaved that they had changed.

Suggest ways the story can have relevance for all. This should be done in such a way that pupils are free to find personal relevance in the story if they wish. Example: think quietly for a moment about times when you have been sorry and how you showed that you had changed.

Stages 1 and 2 are initial teacher planning stages. The pupils' first learning experience is of something which is relevant to them at stage 3. Further ideas for stories and themes which can be used at stage 4 of the planning process can be found on pages 27–30, *Story and Drama*.

Examples follow of how this same approach can be used on a single story such as Ruth or on a festival such as Christmas.

Concept cracking a story: Ruth

Stage 1: Unpack the idea
The story of Ruth is about commitment and God's care in adversity. It's a story of love and faithfulness.

Stage 2: Select one idea to follow up
Example: Commitment.

Stage 3: Engage with the pupils' experience
Talk about the pupils' commitment to their friends.
When is loyalty difficult?

Stage 4: Religious and relevant
Introduce the biblical material and make it relevant.
Tell the story of Ruth. Explore it using techniques such as "Conversations" page 53, *Story and Drama*.

Relevance
Relate a modern story of Christian commitment or explore the marriage service.
Ask pupils to think about people to whom they are committed.

Concept cracking a festival: Christmas

With a festival, there is one stage prior to unpacking – this can be likened to creating a "jigsaw". If a festival is imagined to be like a jigsaw picture, made up of many parts, then a different piece of the "jigsaw" can be covered each year. Examples of jigsaws for Christmas, Easter, Pentecost and Harvest are given overleaf.

Christmas

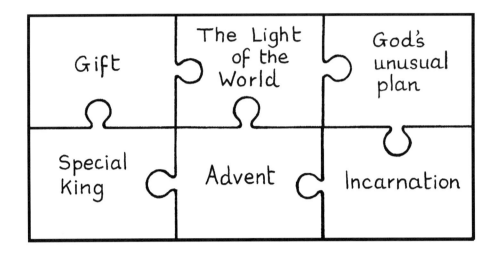

Gift (God's gift of Jesus – John 3.16; the wise men's gifts – Matthew 2.11)

The light of the world (John 1.9; 8.12; 12.35–36)

God's unusual plan (God's choice of a poor couple in an occupied land)

The special king (Messiah – Isaiah 9.1–7; 11.1–9; Luke 1.67–79)

Advent (waiting in hope, prophecy – Isaiah 7.14; Micah 5.2)

Incarnation (Immanuel "God with us" – Matthew 1.18–23, Hebrews 4.15–16)

Easter

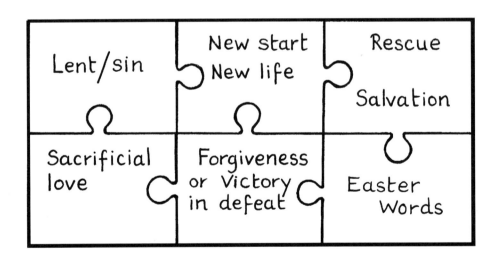

Lent (preparation for Easter, spiritual spring-clean)

New start, new life (life-out-of-death symbolism; people who started a new life after meeting Jesus)

Sin (the adulterous woman – John 8.1–11, all have done wrong) (older pupils)

Rescue, salvation (Noah as an example of rescue; Jesus rescues from sin)

Forgiveness (Jesus on the cross, the dying thief)

Victory in defeat (resurrection after death)

Sacrificial love (dying for others)

Easter words ("atonement" – covering or erasing wrong, and similar)

Pentecost (celebrating the Holy Spirit)

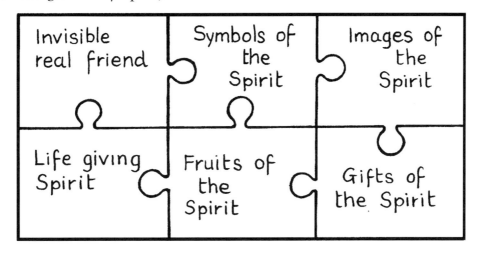

An invisible but real friend (John 14.25–27)

The symbols of the Holy Spirit (wind, fire – Acts 2; dove – Matthew 3.13–17)

The images of the Holy Spirit (comforter, counsellor – John 14.16; 15.26)

The gifts of the Spirit (1 Corinthians 12)

The fruits of the Spirit (Galatians 5.22, 23)

Life-giving Spirit (Genesis 1.2; 2.7; Ezekiel 37.1–14; John 3.1–21)

Harvest

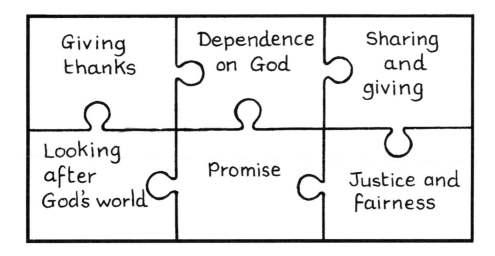

Giving thanks (Psalm 136.1–9; the story of the ten lepers – Luke 17.11–19)

Dependence on God (God the provider – the Israelites in the wilderness – Exodus 16.1–36)

Sharing and giving (the story of Ruth – Book of Ruth; the widow's gift – Luke 21.1–4; the rich fool – Luke 12.13–21)

Looking after God's world (creation – Genesis 1 and 2)

Promise (Noah – Genesis 8.22)

Justice and fairness (inequalities in sharing; relief agencies; biblical laws on just treatment of the poor – Deuteronomy 10.19; 15.7; 24.17; Luke 14.13; James 5.1–5)

Where a festival is based on a particular story, the whole story will be told each time but a different aspect will be highlighted each year. Approaching festivals in this way ensures both continuity and progression as the students' understanding develops over the years of schooling. Having prepared the jigsaw the concept cracking methodology is then applied to the particular piece of the jigsaw to be taught. An example follows.

Christmas: God's unusual plan

Stage 1: Unpack the idea
The choice of Mary. Jesus born into a poor Jewish family.
The poor circumstances of the birth. Making plans.

Stage 2: Select one idea to follow up
The choice of Mary.

Stage 3: Engage with the pupils' experience
Give the pupils the opportunity to make choices and ask them to justify why they chose as they did.

Stage 4: Religious and relevant
Introduce biblical material and make it relevant.
Tell the story of the annunciation. Use the "Stolen picture" activity on page 42, *Art and Music* for this. Other biblical characters who were not obvious choices can be explored: Gideon, David, Moses, Jeremiah.

Relevance
Look at the life of a modern Christian such as Mother Teresa. Would they have been an obvious choice?
  Ask pupils to think about their own choices. Do they always make the obvious choices? Do they need to look closer at people and see the hidden potential?
A booklet entitled *Concept Cracking: Exploring Christian Beliefs in Schools* giving further details of this process is available from Stapleford House, Wesley Place, Stapleford, Notts. NG9 8DP.

THE THREE Es

When using activities from these books, it is important to be clear about their purpose. Activities have three roles:

- To engage. They engage a pupil's interest and earth the subject in the child's world.
- To explore. They help pupils explore the meaning and significance of a subject.
- To express. They help pupils express their own understanding of a subject after due exploration.

Sometimes an activity can have more than one purpose. Here is an example of how one activity can be used to fulfil the three different purposes.

- Engage.   Give the pupils three faces from a local newspaper, then ask them to select one face and say what may have happened to create the expression (choose with care).
- Explore.   To explore the story of Moses and the bulrushes, give the pupils the three faces below. Tell the pupils they are all the same character. Ask them to suggest which character it is, what each face expresses, and why the character feels that way.
- Express.   Give the pupils freedom to choose any character from the story at any moment. Ask them to draw or describe what they think that person's expression would be and why they felt that way.

EXPLORING RELIGIOUS IDEAS

The arts can be used to explore religious ideas which are often thought of as too difficult for children. The expressive nature of the arts means they can often carry ideas that are beyond analysis intellectually. Through dance, art, and poetry, pupils can "catch a feel" of things they may not fully understand. For example, the central belief in the Christmas story is called INCARNATION – a big word which understandably deters most teachers. Some of the ideas contained within this Christian belief are:

God with us (Matthew 1.23; Hebrews 4.15–16)

The incarnation (the word literally means "in flesh") is God's son becoming one of us. It has been described as "God with skin on"! The word Immanuel simply means "God with us". It is God's son sharing human life, knowing what it is like to be human: what it means to laugh and to cry, to have friends and to be rejected. As a result of this doctrine, Christians believe people can pray feeling confident they will be understood, as Jesus knows the trials and joys of being human.

Giving up power (Philippians 2.5–9)

Becoming one of us meant giving up power and control. It meant facing poverty and danger. It was the creator becoming part of his own creation. (Christians believe Jesus, God, and the Holy Spirit were all involved in creation.)

The purpose of the incarnation (John 3.16)

The purpose of the incarnation was to rescue or save. Christians see Jesus as a baby with a mission, someone who came to change the situation and show people what God is like by his teaching and the way he lived.

Ways of exploring the incarnation using the arts

- The idea of giving up power
  Explore what it would be like for the teacher or head teacher to start in the infants. What would s/he have to give up? What would s/he miss? This can be done verbally as a discussion, as an interview, or as a written exercise. Christians believe that Jesus is God's son and gave up many things to come to earth to share our lives.

- Giving up control

    The incarnation is the creator becoming part of his own creation. It is an author becoming part of his or her own book, subject to the plot and all the conditions that prevail within the story. An author is outside the story, in control, safe. A character is not safe: they can be in danger, as Jesus was. Look through some story books with the pupils and decide which character they would be if "sucked" into the book. What conditions would they have to endure? What dangers would they be in? Christians believe Jesus willingly became part of his own creation because he loved people. He became part of our story, subject to its dangers. This can be done as a storytelling or writing activity.

- The creator becoming part of his own creation

    This can be done visually through art. Use dark frieze paper and create a night sky with stars, planets, and so on. In the heart of this, paint a crib scene, or use the night sky as the background to the nativity figures. Underneath have the words of a carol such as "Lo, within a manger lies he who made the starry skies" from "See amid the winter's snow".

- What it's like to be me

    Pupils can write about themselves and try to communicate "What it is like to be me". Give the pupils specific items to write about, so that it is not too intrusive: likes, hates, what it is like to be ten years old, for example. The incarnation is about "God in our shoes". Christians believe God's son became one of us and understands what it is like to be human, and that therefore he understands when people pray.

- Being human

  Christians believe Jesus knew what it was like to be human but with one
  important exception: he did no wrong. He knew what it was like to be tempted,
  to laugh, and to cry. These emotions can be communicated in dance or drama,
  or simple masks can be used made from paper plates showing the different
  expressions.

- Sharing

  We can share many things – money, time, toys. Pupils can play sharing games, or
  talk about the different things that can be shared. Christians believe that God
  shared what was most important to him – his son. They believe that Jesus shared
  our human life and knows what it is like to be human.

- Purpose

  Pupils can explore the idea of having a special mission. This can be done in the
  "secret agent" role-play format. The pupils become the agents who are given all
  sorts of missions on slips of paper by the teacher or leader. When the leader of
  the meeting has left, the agents get together to discuss who has the most difficult
  mission before they leave to start their assignments. Christians believe Jesus
  came with a special, very difficult, mission, to show people what God is like. He
  did this by the things he taught, and by the way he lived and died.

- The most special baby

  Young pupils can start by contrasting special and ordinary. Create a special
  display: special clothes, objects, toys. Talk about special people. For Christians,
  Jesus was the most special baby ever because they believe he was God's son.

WRITING

INTRODUCTION

Background

The Bible contains many different types of writing, originally written for a variety of purposes. There are stories, laws, advice and parables. There are prophecies, teaching passages, poems, history and songs. Most of the New Testament and much of the Old Testament is written in prose, though distinguishing poetry from prose is not always easy in the Bible.

In the beginning, when God created the universe, the earth was formless and desolate. The raging ocean that covered everything was engulfed in total darkness, and the Spirit of God was moving over the water.
Genesis 1.1–2

Christians have always written to express their beliefs. Some Christians express their faith in letters as Paul did in the Bible. Others express their belief in formal writing on doctrine, or in imaginative writing such as the novel. Faith expressed in prose is neither dull nor unimaginative. The written form of the Bible, particularly the Authorized Version of 1611, has been a major influence on the culture of the British Isles. This influence has left British literature full of references to the Bible and biblical images.

As a major vehicle of the Christian faith, prose has obvious advantages in RE.

• Certain forms of writing raise the awareness of pupils, which is essential in RE. They can help to develop empathy and understanding.
• Creative forms of writing can invite pupils to see a subject from an unusual angle. They can make them think and can stimulate discussion.
• The creative process involved in writing encourages response, decision making, and analysis, all vital elements in RE.
• Writing can be a channel for expressing religious ideas in a safe context where pupils will not be ridiculed. Secular society does not give people a context for expressing this side of life.
• The metaphors and similes used in writing help pupils understand religious language, which is rich in metaphor, analogy, and simile.
• Writing can help some pupils express their own thoughts and feelings. It also enables them to explore a biblical character's perspective. For some, the mechanics of writing will be difficult, others will be frustrated by their lack of ability to express what they want to say in words. This is not a case for avoiding writing: it is a case for developing basic skills and alternative methods, such as using computers, in order to free pupils to express their ideas.
• Creative forms of writing enable pupils to engage with the Bible in an "affective" way.

There are some techniques which are too affective, however, to use with certain RE content (for example the crucifixion). Teachers need to select subjects for creative techniques sensitively.

On the whole, people tend to use stories rather than the other types of writing. This preference is reflected in the biblical references in this book, but there are also some suggestions for using non-story material.

A number of techniques are included in the activity section which will help develop pupils' writing skills. To give pupils a blank sheet of paper without a structure for their writing is to invite the mind to go similarly blank!

Resources

Books
General

Real Writing by J Foggin (Hodder & Stoughton, 1992)

The Essential Guide to Writing by C Webster (Folens, 1994)

Developing English: Approaches with IT (NATE, 1993)

Planning for Language by W Lynch (NCET, 1991)

The Integrated Classroom: Language, Learning and IT by P Moore and S Tweddle (Hodder & Stoughton, 1992)

Bright Ideas English by J Holderness (Scholastic, 1993)

Bright Ideas Imaginative Writing by W Magee (Scholastic, 1994)

Words with Wings by M Andrews (Belair, 1991)

Bright Ideas Writing by D Wray (Scholastic, 1988)

Inspirations for Writing by S Ellis and G Friel (Scholastic, 1991)

How to be Brilliant at Writing Stories by I Yates (Brilliant Publications, 1993)

Practical Approaches to Writing by M A Bean and P Wagstaff (Longman, 1991)

Brain Waves, Creative Writing, Lower Junior and Upper Junior by P and S Harrison (Scholars Town, 1989)

Brain Waves, Writing for Different Purposes, Level 1 and 2 by P and S Harrison (Scholars Town, 1989)

Developing Children's Writing edited by J Hammond (Scholastic, 1988)

Christian writings

The list here would be endless. I have included a few anthologies for the classroom.

Pocket Christmas by N and H Whitehead (Church House Publishing/National Society, 1995)

Words For Easter by P Egan (Church House Publishing, 1990). An anthology of Easter poetry and prose.

The Lion Book of Christian Classics by V Zundel (Lion, 1985)

Useful addresses

NATE
(National Association for the Teaching of English)
50 Broadfield Road,
Broadfield Business Centre,
Sheffield,
S8 0XJ.

NCET
(National Council of Education Technology)
Sir William Lyons Road,
Science Park,
University of Warwick,
Coventry,
CV4 7EZ.

Writing in the Bible

There are various types of writing in the Bible: laws, letters, history, wisdom, apocalyptic literature, poetry and song. They were each written for a different purpose. Some activities are more suitable for older pupils while younger pupils can do part of an activity. The activities in this section are specific to the examples used.

Letters

Philemon 1–4

From Paul, a prisoner for the sake of Christ Jesus, and from our brother Timothy –

To our friend and fellow-worker Philemon, and the church that meets in your house, and our sister Apphia, and our fellow-soldier Archippus:

May God our Father and the Lord Jesus Christ give you grace and peace.

Brother Philemon, every time I pray, I mention you and give thanks to my God.

This is the opening of Paul's letter to Philemon written by Paul when he was in prison. This basic start to a letter contains information about the early church which can be unpacked. The church has no purpose-built building. Paul greets men and women. Christians call each other brother and sister and see God as a father. Paul talks of a "fellow soldier". Presumably he called himself a soldier but in what army and what was he fighting?

Activity

Pupils could be asked a series of questions about this letter.

How does Paul open his letter?
Who does Paul say wrote the letter with him? (We know Paul often dictated letters.)
Where does the local church meet? Why do you think they met there?

What does Paul pray about concerning Philemon?
How do you start letters?
Paul usually includes a "blessing". Look at verse three. Find other blessings in Paul's letters in:

Romans 1.7
Philippians 1.2
Colossians 1.2
Titus 1.4
1 Timothy 1.2
2 Thessalonians 1.2

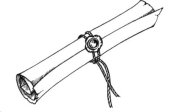

What words are common to them all?
"Grace" means undeserved love. Peace is not just a quiet life, but when life and relationships are "right". Why do you think Paul wished them these two things? What do you wish people when you write to them?

Poetry

Job 28.1–4; 13–15

There are mines where silver is dug;
There are places where gold is refined.
Miners dig iron out of the ground
And melt copper out of
    the stones.
They explore the deepest
    darkness.
They search the depths of
    the earth
And dig for rocks in the
    darkness.
Far from where anyone lives
Or human feet ever travel,
They dig the shafts of
    mines.
There they work in
loneliness,
Clinging to ropes in the pits.

Wisdom is not to be found among mortals;

No one knows its true value.
The depths of the oceans and seas
Say that wisdom is not found there.
It cannot be bought with silver or gold.

This poem from the Book of Job is about mining and wisdom. The poet describes the lengths to which people go in order to find precious stones and gold in the depths of the earth, but asks, "Is not wisdom even rarer than gold and silver?" Wisdom in the Bible is not just intellectual cleverness. Wisdom is about living in right relationships with God and others.

Activity

What is the message of this poem?

Do people still spend most of their efforts on getting wealth?

What do people consider to be more important in life – wealth or relationships?

Think of one practical way in which a person could show that people and God are more important than wealth.

Wisdom
Proverbs 24.1–2

Don't be envious of evil people, and don't try to make friends with them. Causing trouble is all they ever think about; every time they open their mouth someone is going to be hurt.

Wisdom is practical advice for living. Much of it can be found in the Book of Proverbs and in Ecclesiastes, but there are pieces of wisdom scattered throughout the Bible.

Activity

How practical is this piece of advice today?

How could it apply in school?

Look through some of the advice given in Chapter

20 of the Book of Proverbs. Find one other piece of advice that you think still applies and describe when you might use it.

NOTE: with younger pupils teachers can give them a selection of verses from Chapter 20.

Apocalyptic writing
Revelation 22.1–2

The angel also showed me the river of the water of life, sparkling like crystal, and coming from the throne of God and of the Lamb and flowing down the middle of the city's street. On each side of the river was the tree of life, which bears fruit twelve times a year, once each month; and its leaves are for the healing of the nations.

Apocalyptic literature is often written in picture language: it is heavily coded and full of symbols. The Books of Daniel and Ezekiel in the Old Testament and the Book of Revelation in the New Testament contain much apocalyptic writing, but there are also apocalyptic passages spread throughout the Bible. Reading apocalyptic literature is like cracking a code when someone has lost the key! This passage is part of a description of heaven.

Activity

A lamb sits on the throne in this passage. Who or what do you think the lamb stands for? What type of king would have a lamb as his symbol?

What do the tree and the river suggest about heaven?

What do the leaves of the tree suggest?

What needs to be healed between nations?

History

Ezra 6.1–5

So Darius the emperor issued orders for a search to be made in the royal records that were kept in Babylon. But it was in the city of Ecbatana in the province of Media that a scroll was found, containing the following record:

"In the first year of his reign Cyrus the emperor commanded that the Temple in Jerusalem be rebuilt as a place where sacrifices are made and offerings are burnt. The Temple is to be 27 metres high and 27 metres wide. The walls are to be built with one layer of wood on top of every three layers of stone. All expenses are to be paid by the royal treasury. Also the gold and silver utensils which King Nebuchadnezzar brought to Babylon from the Temple in Jerusalem are to be returned to their proper place in the Jerusalem Temple."

The history books (such as Samuel, Kings, Chronicles, Ezra and Nehemiah) tell the story of the people of Israel's relationship with God, and how that was worked out in history. There is also New Testament history of the Church in the Book of Acts. The following extract from the Cyrus cylinder refers to the Israelites being allowed to go home (about 539BC) after they had spent many years in exile under the Babylonians. The Cyrus cylinder, now in the British Museum, confirms that Cyrus did send exiles back, including the Israelites; he also aided the restoration of temples.

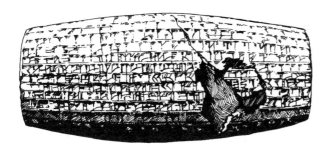

I returned to [these] sacred cities on the other side of the Tigris, the sanctuaries of which have been in ruins for a long time, the image which [used] to live therein and established for them permanent sanctuaries. I [also] gathered all their [former] inhabitants and returned [to them] their habitations.

The Cyrus cylinder, 538BC

Activity
Read the extract from the Cyrus cylinder. Compare it with the extract from Ezra. How much of Ezra does it confirm?

Law

Leviticus 19.11–16

"*Do not steal or cheat or lie.* Do not make a promise in my name if you do not intend to keep it; that brings disgrace on my name. I am the LORD your God.

"*Do not take advantage of anyone or rob him.* Do not hold back the wages of someone you have hired, not even for one night. Do not curse a deaf man or put something in front of a blind man so as to make him stumble over it. Obey me; I am the LORD your God.

"*Be honest and just when you make decisions in legal cases;* do not show favouritism to the poor or fear the rich. Do not spread lies about anyone, and when someone is on trial for his life, speak out if your testimony can help him. I am the LORD."

There are many laws in the Old Testament, the most well known being the Ten Commandments in Deuteronomy 5 and Exodus 20. Often the law gives a basic command and then explains it with examples.

Activity
Look at the quotation from Leviticus. It contains (in the author's italics) basic commands followed by examples of how they would work out in daily life. For example: "Don't rob anyone" works out in practice as "not holding back a person's wages".

Pupils can take some of the basic commands and match them to practical examples in the text or write a practical modern example of not stealing, lying, taking advantage, such as this:

Give things back when you borrow them.

Prophecy
Isaiah 43.5–6

"Do not be afraid – I am with you! From the distant east and the farthest west, I will bring your people home. I will tell the north to let them go and the south not to hold them back. Let my people return from distant lands, from every part of the world."

Micah 6.8

No, the LORD has told us what is good. What he requires of us is this: to do what is just, to show constant love, and to live in humble fellowship with our God.

Prophecy is not only about foretelling the future, it is also about proclaiming God's standards. These two passages show the twin aspects of prophecy.

The first predicts, in poetic form, the return of the scattered children of Israel to their homes. The second tells of God's standards of behaviour.

Activity
Generally we have to live without knowing the future. Prophecy tends to be in general terms, not a daily detailed prediction for each individual. Think of one way in which not knowing in great detail what the future holds helps us.

Gospel
Luke 4.16–20

Then Jesus went to Nazareth, where he had been brought up, and on the Sabbath he went as usual to the synagogue. He stood up to read the Scriptures and was handed the book of the prophet Isaiah. He unrolled the scroll and found the place where it was written:

"The Spirit of the Lord is upon me, because he has chosen me to bring good news to the poor. He has sent me to proclaim liberty to the captives and recovery of sight to the blind; to set free the oppressed and announce that the time has come when the Lord will save his people."

Jesus rolled up the scroll, gave it back to the attendant, and sat down. All the people in the synagogue had their eyes fixed on him.

The word "gospel" literally means "good news". All four "gospels" are the good news about Jesus: his birth, his life, his death and resurrection.

Activity

Look at the passage Jesus read at Nazareth. What items in this would be considered "good news"?

Look at a suitable newspaper. Find three stories which are mainly good news.

What type of stories are considered good news today?

Parable
Luke 7.36–50 (an extract)

"There were two men who owed money to a moneylender," Jesus began. "One owed him five hundred silver coins, and the other owed him fifty. Neither of them could pay him back, so he cancelled the debts of both. Which one, then, will love him more?"

"I suppose," answered Simon, "that it would be the one who was forgiven more."

"You are right," said Jesus … "whoever has been forgiven little shows only a little love."

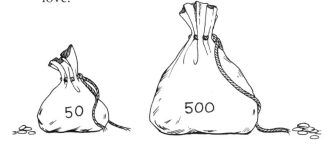

There are many parables in the New Testament and some in the Old Testament.

A parable is a story which usually has one main point. It is not a factual story, though it carries a message. Parables were effective because they took a roundabout route to deliver their message. Would a lecture on loving your neighbour be as effective as the parable of the Good Samaritan?

Activity

What is the message of this parable? Sum it up in one sentence or catchphrase.

Older pupils might want to look at the parable of the sheep told by Nathan in 2 Samuel 12.1–14. The background to this parable is that David (who had a number of wives) took another man's only wife. This is a classic example of how a parable works. Nathan uses a parable to get the king to condemn himself. By using a parable, Nathan sets up a trap – and David falls into it.

Teaching
Luke 11.9–13

"And so I say to you: ask, and you will receive; seek, and you will find; knock, and the door will be opened to you. For all those who ask will receive, and those who seek will find, and the door will be opened to anyone who knocks. Would any of you who are fathers give your son a snake when he asks for fish? Or would you give him a scorpion when he asks for an egg? Bad as you are, you know how to give good things to your children. How much more, then, will the Father in heaven give the Holy Spirit to those who ask him!"

This section comes from Jesus' teaching on prayer which starts at the beginning of chapter 11 and includes the Lord's Prayer.

Activity

If the father in this teaching stands for God, what is Jesus saying about God's attitude to people praying?

The languages of the Bible

The original language of the Old Testament is Hebrew, though some parts are written in Aramaic. The original language of the New Testament is Greek, though the people of Palestine, including Jesus, spoke Aramaic. Greek was a second language for many people: it was the language of culture and business and was used by Christians so that the maximum number of people could read the Bible.

This is the word LOVE written in the original languages of the Bible

Hebrew

חֶסֶד *(hesed)*

Greek

ἀγάπη *(agapē)*

Hebrew: Genesis 1.1

אֵת הַשָּׁמַיִם וְאֵת הָאָרֶץ׃

the-earth   and   the-heavens   ...

בְּרֵאשִׁית בָּרָא אֱלֹהִים

God   he-created   in-beginning

Activity

Give pupils a copy of the Hebrew writing. It is read from right to left. Translated it reads:

> In the beginning God created the heavens and the earth.

These are the opening words of the Bible.

Why do you think the writer chose to open the Bible story with these words?

How do you like to start your writing?

Greek: Revelation 22.21

Ἡ χάρις τοῦ κυρίου Ἰησοῦ μετὰ ᶠπάντων

Activity

Give pupils a copy of the Greek. Translated it reads.

> May the grace of the Lord Jesus be with everyone.

These are the last words of the Bible. The word "grace" means undeserved love.

Why do you think the Bible ends with these words?

How do you like to end your writing?

Twenty-five writing activities

These activities can be used with biblical stories or passages, or with fiction on a biblical theme.

(1) Poetry and prose
Change biblical prose into poetry or poetry into prose. Compare the two versions. Which is more effective? The story of Deborah in Judges 4 and 5 is a good example of the same story told in prose and poetry. NOTE: Samples of biblical poems are given on page 86.

(2) Retelling
The retelling of a story in the pupils' own words can be a creative experience, especially if they have to think carefully about the audience who will receive it, and the context. It may be for publication within the school. It could be for younger children.

(3) Visitors
Invite a Christian writer into school to read something from their own work and ask them how the Bible has influenced their writing.

(4) Masks
Masks can be made to accompany pupils' writing, reflecting the various feelings present. They can also reflect the feelings of people in a piece of writing or biblical story. If the masks are kept fairly plain the writing can be done on the masks themselves.

(5) Decisions
Ask pupils to read a story and locate moments of decision. Pupils should write about the decision, the consequences and what they think might have happened if the character had chosen differently.

(6) Magazine
Pupils can write articles or stories based on biblical material for a class magazine. This would be particularly appropriate at Christmas or Easter.

(7) Discussion
Read a passage from the Bible which deals with an issue; for example Deuteronomy 5.12 concerns a day of rest. Divide the class into pairs to discuss it. Each pair should share their results with another pair and a summary should be made of each group's discussion. Results of these discussions can be written and reported back.

(8) Booklets and guides
Booklets, pamphlets and magazines can be published by pupils using a suitable computer program. Pupils might like to help with a church magazine in conjunction with a local church. They could also compile a guide to local churches and Christian activities in the area. This could form part of a local study, and relate the work of the Church to biblical teaching about the Church.

(9) Good points and bad points
After reading a story, ask pupils to write what they liked about it and what they disliked.

(10) Painting
Look at a painting of a biblical picture such as *Belshazzar's Feast* and write about the story behind it, exploring the artist's interpretation of that story (see page 26, *Art and Music*)

(11) Biographies
Pupils can write short biographies of biblical characters, local Christians, or famous Christians.

(12) Music
Select pieces of music to go with writing. This can be played beforehand or the text can be read over the top of it. For longer stories, such as Joseph, Moses and David, theme music can be written and the stories can be broken up and written as episodes in a soap opera. When the episodes are read the theme music can be played.

(13) Sound effects

Pupils can rewrite a biblical story and then indicate sound effects which could be added.

(14) Shape presentation

Writing can be presented on a three-dimensional mount such as a cube. For example, a multi-sided shape can be created, and pupils' writing on different aspects of Jesus could be pasted on each facet (shepherd, door, etc.).

(15) Lists

Encourage the pupils to keep a list of important things they want to include in their writing. This could be a list formed after discussion, a list made after research, or a list created from a Bible story. Creating the list can be a specific task. If they are asked to rewrite a Bible story, ask the pupils to write a list of the most important facts, feelings and significant points which they must include in their story.

(16) Relay

Pupils can write in relay on a subject. One pupil carrying on where the previous one finished.

(17) Writing scripts

Pupils can write a script for a slide presentation on creation which uses a rewritten version of Genesis 1—2. They can also translate the narrative into a play or a play script. The Dramatised Bible (Marshall Pickering/Bible Society, 1989) lays out the Bible in this form.

(18) Writing backwards

Pupils can try starting at the end of a story and retelling it as if a character is remembering.

(19) Words

Ask pupils to list five significant words from a biblical story they have read. Pupils should be able to write a justification of their choice.

(20) Favourites

Invite a Christian into school to read their favourite pieces of writing from the Bible. Visitors can be questioned by the pupils or they can explain what it means to them.

(21) Letters

Give pupils time to write a letter to a Christian writer asking him or her about their work and how the Bible influences them. Formal letter writing can be taught for this activity.

(22) Alternatives

Write alternative endings to a story. Give the pupils the central part of a story, ask them to write what went before and what happened afterwards. If using a Bible story, use an unfamiliar one.

(23) Tapes

Create a tape of a biblical story rewritten by the pupils so that it can be played to another class or used in an assembly.

(24) Questions

If you could interview the main character in a piece of writing, what would you ask him or her? Write a list of the questions you would ask.

(25) Perspectives

Write an account of the main character as if written by a friend or parent.

Bubbles

Gideon: Judges 6.1—7.25
The man with the withered hand: Matthew 12.9–14
The parable of the two sons: Matthew 21.28–32

Description of the activity
Speech bubbles and thought bubbles are bubbles which are drawn above a character to indicate what they are thinking or saying. Pupils are used to this technique as it is widely used in comics. Bubbles are useful for exploring characters' reactions and thoughts. Speech and thought bubbles can be used together, so that pupils can see that what a character says is not always the same as what they think.

An example
Speech and thought bubbles on the story of the two sons

Geoffrey Yeomans, Year 3, Albany Junior School, Stapleford

Biblical application

This can be used on a large number of stories, but works best when there is conflict, confusion, an unusual instruction, or a difference of opinion involved. In the story of Gideon, the men must have really wondered what Gideon was doing. Gideon himself was really puzzled that God had chosen him. In the parable of the two sons, the boys change their minds, and this change can be represented by bubbles. In the story of the man with the withered hand the bystanders' thoughts can be presented in bubbles. These stories all provide scope for exploring thoughts and feelings.

Points of view

Esau sells his birthright: Genesis 25.27–34
Jacob tricks Isaac: Genesis 27.1–29
Martha and Mary: Luke 10.38–42

Description of the activity

This activity requires the pupils to tell the same story from a number of points of view. Once the pupils have heard the story, they make a list of the characters. Pupils need to be in groups containing the same number of pupils as there are characters. In the case of Esau's birthright, the pupils work in pairs. The story of Jacob's trick involves groups of four. The characters are written separately on pieces of paper and placed in a "hat". Pupils select a piece of paper and write the story from that person's point of view.

An example

The Good Samaritan

The traveller's story

I started travelling down the long road towards Jericho. When I was about half way down the dusty road some robbers jumped out in front and behind me. I felt a short pain rush through my head before everything went dark and blank.

When I woke up everything was fuzzy and I felt dizzy. My vision was not stable as I tried to stand up. I was in a daze. Blood was gushing from several deep cuts. The worst one was on the back of my head where the blood felt slimy and sticky. I fell down onto the dusty road, my whole body felt like jelly. I suddenly "came back to life" with a jerk, my eyes opened and I could see properly. I had been robbed of everything I had had with me. My clothes had been torn into shreds, they were hanging off me like limp bits of cloth. I could not walk another few miles to Jericho.

I looked up and saw a traveller. The traveller was alone. To my great joy, I saw he was a priest. A priest would surely come to my aid. I watched as he crossed to the other side of the road and pretended he had not seen me. I was devastated. I could not call or shout, my whole body was shaking with disbelief. I felt sad and alone. I thought no one would help me and I would die on the long, open road.

When I awoke from a troubled sleep, I saw a small figure in the distance. A few minutes later, I saw the person was a Levite. A Levite is holy. I was sure he would help me. I could not shout because my voice was "caught in my throat". I felt very let down when he crossed the road and ignored me. I was sure now that nobody would help and I would die.

A while later, I saw a figure on horseback approaching. He was a Samaritan, a person of a different nationality. But as he came closer, instead of crossing over he came towards me. The Samaritan got off his donkey and came to me. He cleaned my cuts and wounds and bandaged them as well as he could. When he has done this, the Samaritan picked me up and put me on his donkey. The Samaritan took me to the nearest inn and paid the inn-keeper to look after me. He told him that if I needed more care than the money the Samaritan had given him he would pay on the way back. I was eternally grateful to the "Good Samaritan" as I called him.

Sarah Field, Year 9, Abbey Grange Church of England School, Leeds

Biblical application

This activity works particularly well on stories in which there is a conflict of interests such as in the stories of Martha and Mary, Jacob and Esau, or the money-changers in the Temple (Matthew 21.12–17). It can, however, be used on most stories.

Snatches

Daniel and the food: Daniel 1.1–21
The wedding at Cana: John 2.1–11
The healing of the woman bent double: Luke 13.10–17

Description of the activity

Before telling the story, the teacher writes one sentence which a character in the story *may* have overheard. It is just a snatch from a conversation. The sentence should not be one which actually occurs within the story, but it should be one that fits the characters and events of the story. In the Christmas story, the overheard snatch of conversation could be, "I would never have expected to find him there". The pupils, after listening to the story, decide who could have said this and why. The snatch can become the basis of a discussion. Pupils can try reconstructing the rest of what the character might have said and the response of others. It can be written as a script to avoid the use of quotation marks.

An example

The wedding at Cana

Jesus goes to a wedding

Bridegroom	It's not my fault sir.
Man in charge	Well, it's your wedding sir, you should be the one to blame.
Bridegroom	Oh dear, what shall I do?
Mary	My son will help you, wait here a moment, I shall be back soon.
Jesus	Yes, of course, I will help him Mother.
Mary	Do as my son orders.
Servant	Of course, Madam.
Jesus	Fill the water jugs up and pour them out.
Servant	But we can't do that.
Jesus	Just do it.
Servant	OK, but ...
Man in charge	This wine is beautiful.
Servant	He must be really special.

Laura Shelley, Year 3, Coton Green Primary School, Tamworth

Biblical application

The activity can be used on many Bible stories. The important part for the teacher is designing the sentence which will encourage the pupils to explore the meaning of the story. The snatch of conversation can be presented as a bubble or words drifting from a window or over a wall. If drawn rather than just spoken, it is important that the speaker cannot be seen.

The following snatches are from the wedding at Cana, the woman bent double and Daniel and the food.

Captions

Elijah and the ravens: 1 Kings 17.1–6
Elijah and the widow: 1 Kings 17.7–24
The parable of the sower: Matthew 13.1–23; Mark 4.1–20; Luke 8.4–15

Description of the activity

Captions are short pieces of writing accompanying illustrations which sum up what is happening. There are several ways of using captions.

- Pupils can be given a series of drawings for which they provide the captions. See the example included.

- Pupils can be given a sheet with alternate drawings and blank sections. They have to complete the blank sections.

- They decide the number of episodes a story breaks into and create their own pictures or cartoons plus captions.

An example

Captions for The Good Samaritan

(1) A man was walking from Jerusalem to Jericho.

(2) He was attacked by men, he was stripped and beaten. They left him there half dead.

(3) Then a man saw the man laying there and just carried on walking on the other side. Then another man came and did exactly the same thing as the man before.

(4) Then a Samaritan came and saw the man lying on the road and his heart was filled with pity. He went over and put oil and wine on his wounds and bandaged them.

(5) He put him on his own animal and took him to an inn.

(6) Jesus said we must love our neighbour just as the Samaritan did.

Leah Cooling, Year 4, Binscombe Middle School, Farncombe

Biblical application

This activity can be used on many biblical stories, though some of the longer stories involve too many episodes and take too long to complete. Pupils can write captions for the story of Elijah, using the pictures provided, or they can decide how the parable of the sower breaks up into episodes, and draw their own pictures and captions for each section.

Elijah and the widow

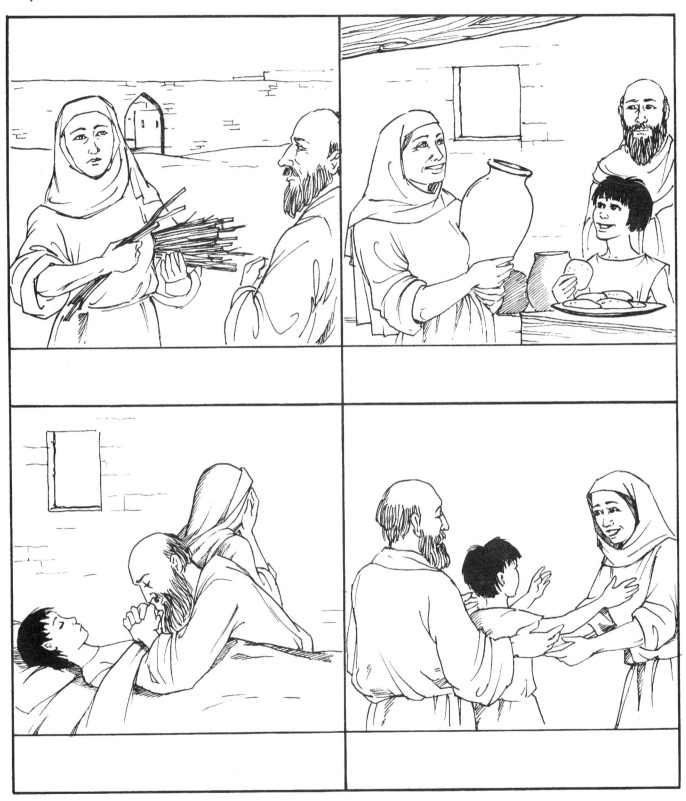

© 1996 Bible Society. This page may be photocopied for classroom use only.

Letters and postcards

David in hiding: 1 Samuel 21.1–23
The prodigal son: Luke 15.11–32
Nehemiah and the wall: Nehemiah 2.11–20; 4.1–23

Description of the activity

Formal letter writing can be a valuable skill to learn: it can also form part of RE. There are various characters within stories who either write to each other or who could have written to each other. Pupils write what they think were the contents of those imaginary letters.

Another form of this technique is for the pupils to write to a character in a story asking them questions. For example, the pupils might write a letter to a character asking how they felt about certain incidents, or their motives for behaving in a particular way.

An example

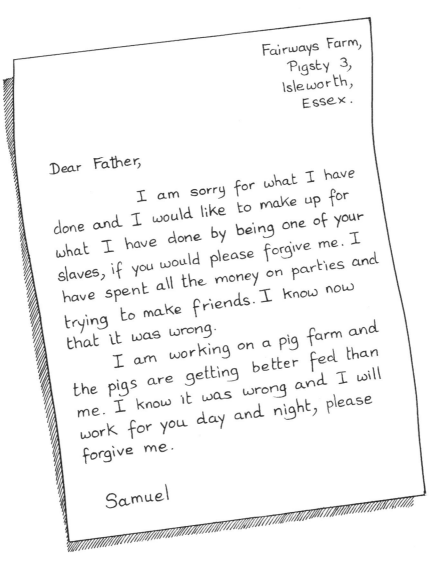

Fairways Farm,
Pigsty 3,
Isleworth,
Essex.

Dear Father,

I am sorry for what I have done and I would like to make up for what I have done by being one of your slaves, if you would please forgive me. I have spent all the money on parties and trying to make friends. I know now that it was wrong.

I am working on a pig farm and the pigs are getting better fed than me. I know it was wrong and I will work for you day and night, please forgive me.

Samuel

Sarah Johnson, Year 5, St John's Church of England Primary School, Stapleford

Biblical application

Letter writing, although a formal skill, can also be used creatively. What might David have written to his family while he was hiding from Saul? If he had written to Saul himself, what might he have said? What would Nehemiah have written to friends back in Babylon? What might the prodigal son have written to his father?

Give the pupils blank postcards, if possible, or paper and envelopes and ask them to write what they think was in one of those imaginary letters. The cards or letters can be placed in their folders or books. Pupils can also write letters to biblical characters asking them to explain their actions, feelings and motives. They might like to write a letter to Saul asking about his treatment of David. Other pupils can attempt to answer as if they were that character.

Emotions dip

Naboth's vineyard: 1 Kings 21.1–29
The Christmas story: Matthew 1.18–25; 2.1–12; Luke 2.1–20
Zacchaeus: Luke 19.1–10

Description of the activity

This technique highlights the various emotional responses in a story. After reading a story to the class, ask them to note the different emotions which occur and who felt them. Pupils do not have to list only the emotions *named* within a story: they can often deduce what people were feeling. For example, it does not say that Joseph was worried in the Christmas story but that is an acceptable deduction.

It is usually necessary to read the story twice to give the pupils time to assess the feelings involved. Once a class list of emotions has been obtained, pupils should, in groups, transfer the emotions on that list to pieces of card or paper so that each group has a set of identical words.

The cards should be placed in a "hat" and from this pupils select one piece of paper each (with their eyes closed). They then rewrite the story bringing out that particular aspect. You may wish to give the pupils a copy of the story at this point.

Pupils write the *whole* story but highlight one emotion as it occurs. They do not have to repeat the word they pulled out of the hat continuously: they can use a thesaurus to find related words which describe the same emotion or suitable word lists can be created. Teachers will need to give pupils a few examples of how this could be done, quickly retelling the story bringing out a particular emotion.

The Christmas story: some of the emotions felt

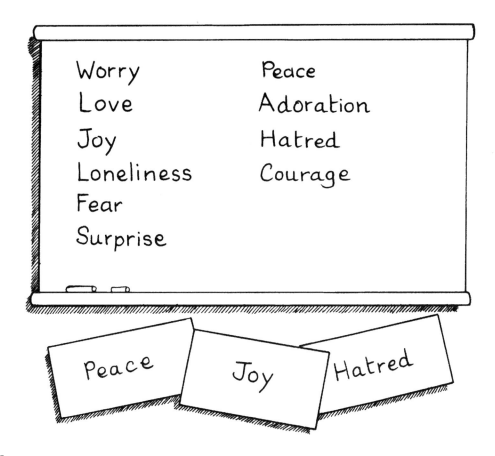

Examples

The obsession

Next to King Ahab's Palace there was a vineyard belonging to a man called Naboth. One day King Ahab had an idea. "I'm going to buy that vineyard and make it the royal garden," he said. But Naboth didn't want to lose it. All the king thought about was the garden. It became an obsession, and he refused to eat or drink. His wife was anxious so she killed Naboth. "He's dead," she said. The land became Ahab's but God knew about the anger and the jealousy so he sent a man to the king to tell him this so that justice was done.

Daniel Williams, Year 6, Stevenson County Junior School, Stapleford

Anger

Opposite King Ahab's palace there was a vineyard that belonged to a man called Naboth. One day Ahab had an idea, "If I owned that vineyard," he thought, "I could really make it into a nice vegetable garden. It would be really handy just there."

He went to Naboth's house and offered to buy it or exchange it for one in a different place, but Naboth didn't want to lose it. "My family has owned this land for years," he said angrily. "I'll keep it," he told the astonished king.

Ahab was furious and angry. How dare the man refuse the king anything! He went home and just lay on his bed and sulked. He even refused to eat anything. When his wife Jezebel came in she laughed at him. "Come on," she jeered. Then she carried out a cruel plot against Naboth.

Nicola Goodhall, Year 5, Stevenson County Junior School, Stapleford

Biblical application

This technique can be used for many stories in the Bible providing a range of emotions are included. The story of Naboth contains envy, the story of Zacchaeus, rejection and acceptance. Christmas and Easter are particularly suitable. This technique allows pupils to explore emotions and reactions present in the story which they may not have noticed before. Time should be given to discussing these – who felt them and why. Careful questioning can also help bring out meaning: "Why was Herod full of hatred?" "What made Joseph worry?"

What the donkey saw

The feeding of the five thousand: Matthew 14.13–21; Mark 6.30–44; Luke 9.10–17; John 6.1–15
The baptism of Jesus: Matthew 3.13–17; Mark 1.9–11; Luke 3.21, 22; John 1.29–34
The transfiguration: Matthew 17.1–13; Mark 9.2–13; Luke 9.28–36

Description of the activity

This activity involves an animal, imported into the story, which retells it adding its own comments and questions. Once the pupils have heard the story, ask them to invent a creature which would fit in, but does not actually occur within the story. For example, it could be a fish or a donkey, a bird or a grasshopper.

The story is retold by this animal, which, because it has no integral role to play, is free to recount the events and comment on the behaviour of the people. Younger pupils may like to write within a drawn outline of the creature who is speaking. Another way of displaying this technique is for the writing to be done on the computer. The creature can be drawn using the computer and the writing can be inserted within the outline. The line lengths can be changed to fit inside the drawing.

An example

What the mouse saw

One sunny day when the sky was blue I came out of my hole.
    What a peaceful day just lying in the sun, then I heard a lot of chattering. "George, George" I said.
    "What now" he said sleepily.
    "There's that man again."
    Just then he [the man] said to all the people to sit down on the grass, so the people did as they were told...
    A little boy came up to the disciples and said "I have five loaves and two fishes if these people are hungry," so Jesus took the five loaves and two fishes and looked up to heaven and said thank you to God. He told the people to divide into groups and everyone ate and had enough.
    Then my husband came inside and told me the whole story.

Tina Clough, Year 4, St John's Church of England Primary School, Stapleford

Biblical application

This activity is very versatile and can be used on most biblical stories. Pupils can choose to be a flea on the knee of a wise man's camel, or a bird in a bush on the mountain of the transfiguration. In the case of the feeding of the five thousand, they might be a sparrow waiting to pick up crumbs, or an ant in the grass. At the baptism, they could be a heron on the river bank or a donkey waiting nearby. It is important that the animal not only tells the story but also comments and asks questions: Who is this? Why are they...? If the pupils produce a retelling, as above, rather than a comment on the story, teachers can use pupil work as a basis for conversation and questioning. For example "Do you think the mouse believed 'George' when he told her what had happened?"

Reporters and newspapers

The escape from Egypt: Exodus 12.31–42
The arrest of Jesus: Matthew 26.47–56; Mark 14.43–52; Luke 22.47–53; John 18.1–11
The death of John the Baptist: Matthew 14.1–12; Mark 6.14–29; Luke 9.7–9

Description of the activity

Newspaper reports are a useful way of exploring stories and can be used in the classroom. Computer programmes can be used to produce newspaper reports of various incidents. Pupils should read some newspaper stories (choose with care) to become familiar with the reporting style before attempting to write their own. They could also investigate bias in writing, discovering how the same event can be reported in different ways depending on your outlook.

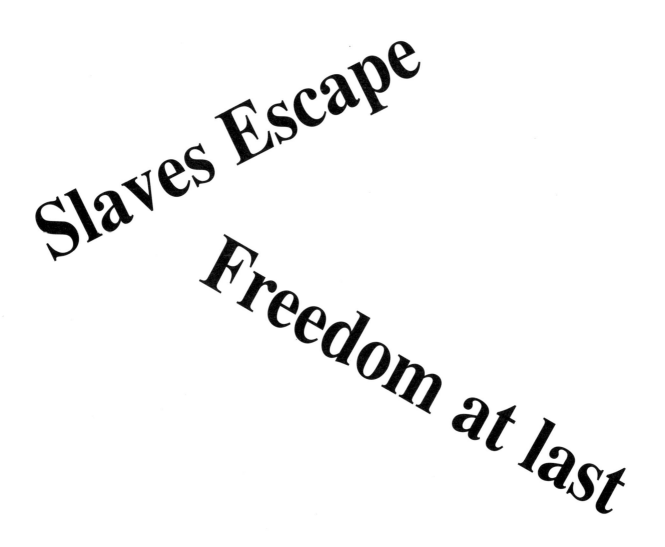

The Jerusalem Times

ALIVE ONE MINUTE DEAD THE NEXT

We are three believers — Apostles. We share everything we own. People who own houses and fields have to sell them and give all the money, received from the sale, to us.

A married couple called Ananias and Sapphira sold some of their land. They both agreed to keep some of the money for themselves and hand the rest over to us. When Ananias came to us to hand the money over, Peter — our leader — went up to him and asked him why he had let Satan rule him and make him lie by keeping part of the money for himself. Peter told Ananias he had "lied to God". As soon as he heard this,

Ananias "fell down dead". The undertakers wrapped him in cloth and buried him. Everyone who heard this was really scared.

Three hours later, Sapphira came along. She did not know about what had happened to Ananias. Peter asked her if this money was the whole amount received from their land. She said it was. Peter then asked her, "Why did you and your

husband decide to put the Lord's Spirit to the test?" The undertakers who buried her husband were standing at the door, ready to take her away. Sapphira fell down and died instantly. The undertakers buried her next to Ananias. All the other people were absolutely terrified.

We have told you this story to help you understand that it is always better to tell the truth than to lie.

Reported by:
Laura Batten
Laura Winson
Elizabeth Hancock

Newcastle-Under-Lyme School. Year 8.

The Jewish Times

Death by Peter!

This community mourns the deaths of two valued citizens but they also fear for their own lives.

Two members of the Christian group who had agreed to share their possessions with other members of the cult were killed yesterday.

Ananias and Sapphira had given all their money and possessions to the group. They eventually decided that they couldn't live on the small amount that was given to them when ever they needed food or clothing. So after selling one of their fields they

Ananias and Sapphira

agreed on keeping some of the money for themselves and giving the rest to the apostles. Peter (leader of the cult) verbally abused him and was about to strike him when the poor man fell down dead. When asking the bereaved mother what she thought of

Peter she said, "I never thought that this good man would do such a thing."

A few hours later Sapphira (who had no knowledge of the recent happenings) went to Peter. Peter verbally abused her as well and then asked if

she was telling the truth on the sale of the field. The last words he spoke to her were, "The men who buried your husband are now at the door and they will carry you out too." On these awful words Sapphira fell down dead. There is no doubt as to who killed them but some people are refusing to believe this horrid murder. The funeral for Ananias and Sapphira will be on 14th Siban.

Reported by Alice Jones and Rebecca Tudor, Newcastle-Under-Lyme School. Year 8.

Biblical application

There are many biblical stories which would have been newsworthy: the escape from Egypt, Jesus throwing out the money-changers (Luke 19.45–48), the entry into Jerusalem (Matthew 21.1–11). Some of these stories can be written from different perspectives. For example, using the story of the escape from Egypt, the pupils can work in pairs and write two accounts: one for the "Egyptian Times" and one for the "Hebrew Herald". The bias and views present in these reports can then be the subject of discussion. The arrest of Jesus could be reported in an official Jewish newspaper and in a popular newspaper favourable towards Jesus. The death of John the Baptist could be afforded similar treatment. A report can be a collaborative effort which is discussed and drawn up by a group.

Board games and quizzes

Some parables of Jesus
The houses built on rock and on sand: Matthew 7.24–27
The two debtors: Luke 7.36–50
The rich fool: Luke 12.13–21
The good Samaritan: Luke 10.25–37
The lost sheep, coin and son: Luke 15
The ten bridesmaids, The talents, and The sheep and the goats: Matthew 25
The treasure and The pearl: Matthew 13.44–46
The friend at midnight: Luke 11.5–13
The sower: Matthew 13.1–23

Description of the activity

The simplest form of this activity involves the pupils listening to a story or stories, and then creating a game in which the pupils can move forwards or backwards depending on their answers. This activity can be done in pairs or groups, and pupils can swap games. The questions should be written first, or pupils may spend so long designing the game that they never get to the questions.

An example

Board game and questions

Q. What does this parable teach the people?

A. Your neighbour is everyone no matter who they are.

Q. Who are the people who are not rich in God's sight?

A. Those who pile up their riches.

Q. How much did the Samaritan give to the innkeeper?

A. 2 silver coins.

Q. What is a parable?

A. A parable is a story told by Jesus to his followers to teach them about God.

Venetia Lamb, Vicky Sessions, Rebecca Wilkins, Year 7, Park School, Yeovil

Biblical application

This example is a parable game. The pupils listen to several parables. They then write a series of questions on those parables, covering not only content but also feelings and meaning. The questions can be weighted, questions of meaning carrying more points than others.

The board should be of a fairly simple design (it can be created on the computer), the emphasis being on the questions. It could be a chequered board where pupils move forwards or backwards according to how they answer the questions. It could have a winding pathway, or players can move through various zones. It could have special squares where pupils pick up extra points if they land on them.

The board game can be a useful way of mastering content. It can be used in conjunction with other techniques which explore meaning, though some exploration of meaning can be conveyed through the questions.

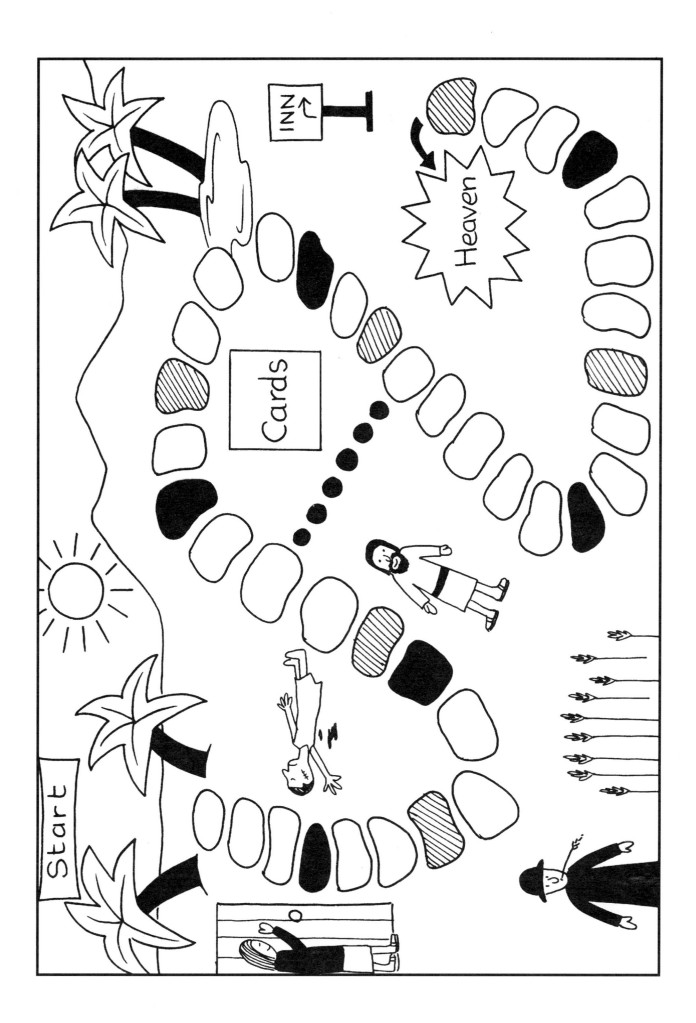

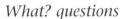

Writing questions

Abraham and Isaac: Genesis 22.1–19 (older pupils)

Ask, seek, knock: Matthew 7.7–12; Luke 11.9–13

Jesus' teaching on prayer: Matthew 6.5–15

Description of the activity

A series of questions can be asked about a story. Questions come in roughly three forms, which can be summed up as:

- "What?" or factual questions
- "Why?" or significance questions
- "So what?" or relevance and affective questions

What? questions

These are factual questions about content (WHAT, HOW, WHO, WHEN, WHERE). They are often "closed" questions, requiring the pupil to search the passage to find the one "right" answer. For example,

> What objects does the son ask for? (Matthew 7.7–12)

Why? questions

These are questions relating to significance and interpretation (WHY). These are often "open" questions, where the pupils look at the passage and interpret it. The open format allows for a range of responses. For example,

> Why do you think Abraham was given this command? (Genesis 22.1–19)

So what? questions

Relevance questions (SO WHAT) should be "open", allowing for a variety of responses. The pupils move out from the passage to application and relevance. For example,

> The Lord's Prayer says "Lead us not into temptation." How do people lead others into temptation today? (Matthew 6.9–13)

Once pupils have learnt these three forms of questions, they can write their own set of questions on a biblical story for another group.

An example

Questions on the unforgiving servant

Matthew 18.21–35

1 How many servants were there in the story?

2 Why do you think the king forgave the servant?

3 What would you do if this happened to you?

Tara Woolley, Matthew Hooton and Oshin Haghoubian, Year 6, Bramcote Hills Primary School, Nottingham

Biblical application

These forms of question can be applied to most passages. Questions should cover all three categories. Teachers can restrict pupils to one question. If pupils were asked to select one question only which they were allowed to ask about this passage or story, what would it be? They should be able to justify their selection.

Trackers

Honesty: Proverbs 11.3; 19.1
Giving: Matthew 5.42
Telling the truth: Ephesians 4.25

Description of the activity
"Choose your own adventure" books are written to a special pattern which allows you to choose what happens to the main character. Many computer programs use the same format. The scenario is set up and the main character is given a number of choices. Each choice has a resulting consequence which leads to other choices. By making a number of choices, a character chooses their own path, creating their own story.

Opening scenario
Pat sees Chris, an unpopular pupil, waiting at the bus stop. Chris is badly shaken and upset. S/he has lost all his/her money and has no money for the bus to school. Do you …

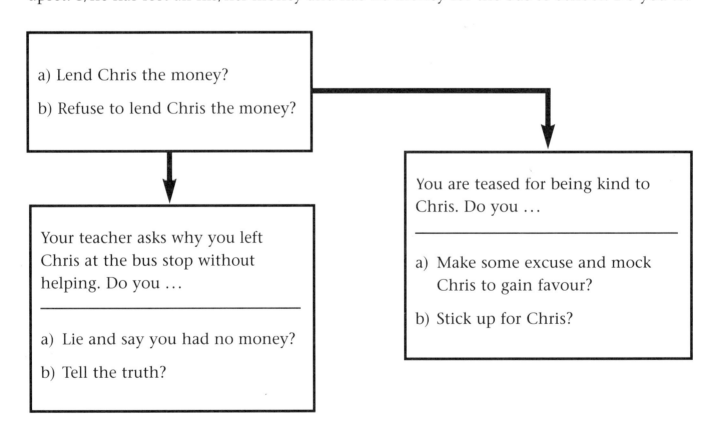

a) Lend Chris the money?

b) Refuse to lend Chris the money?

Your teacher asks why you left Chris at the bus stop without helping. Do you …

a) Lie and say you had no money?

b) Tell the truth?

You are teased for being kind to Chris. Do you …

a) Make some excuse and mock Chris to gain favour?

b) Stick up for Chris?

An example

The exam

> You are sitting in an important exam and you are in early. You see the exam paper sitting at the front. Do you...

> A: Sit there?
>
> B: Make your way slowly to the front of the class?

> The teacher comes in and says how truthful you are. She has to go, so she puts you in charge of the classroom. Are you...

> A: Tempted to take a look?
>
> B: Don't look at it?

> You are alone. Will you turn over the exam paper?

> A: Yes.
>
> B: No.

You have looked through it and discovered that you have left practically all of the revision out. Do you...

A: Go and sit in your seat?

B: Go and make cheat notes on what you haven't got?

You have your revision notes inside the pencil case. When the teacher walks around, she stands beside you and gets suspicious. Do you...

A: Give in the notes?

B: Carry on, don't admit anything?

She walks away and you get out your notes. She turns around and catches you. Do you...

A: Deny everything?

B: Apologise and give her your notes?

Your report comes in and you know there are going to be no marks for that test (your parents don't know about your cheating). Do you...

A: Steam open the letter and fill marks in?

B: Leave it alone and get in trouble with your parents?

Nicola Stewart, Claire Finlay, Form 4, Rainey Endowed School, Magherafelt

Biblical application

These adventure style books can be used in conjunction with the Bible, allowing pupils to explore a biblical point of view. The opening scenario should be a moral dilemma, as in the case of the example given, of a Christian teenager called Pat.

Biblical references (such as the ones beginning this section) should be given as these would form part of Pat's thinking. Pupils should discuss how Pat would feel and what choices s/he would make and how Pat's faith might affect his or her actions. They should then explore the consequences of Pat's actions. Pupils should remember that although Pat may know the Bible's teaching on honesty, that does not mean s/he is never tempted or never goes against his or her conscience. Trackers can be written with boxes and choices as in the example on page 52, or they can be written as simple choices as in the example on page 53–54 where only one set of choices is actually followed up. Pupils may like to create their own scenario or choose from one of the following.

Telling the Truth: You are spotted in town by a friend of your family when you should be at school. Do you tell the truth or lie?

Showing Mercy: Someone who has tormented you for ages suddenly needs your help. (See relevant material in 1 Samuel 24.)

Pillowcase

The healing of Naaman: 2 Kings 5.1–27
The prodigal son: Luke 15.11–32
The good Samaritan: Luke 10.25–37

Description of the activity

There are two forms of this activity

- The teacher places three items in a pillow case which relate in some way to the story she is about to tell. The items chosen may be intrinsic to the story, such as a small bag of earth in the story of Naaman. Alternatively, the items may not occur in the story, but may encourage the pupils to use their imagination, and help to bring out its meaning. For example, there is no mention of a letter in the story of the prodigal son, but it is reasonable to speculate on what he might have written to his father. Therefore a letter could justifiably be one of the items in the pillowcase. Two of the three items can be straightforward and "factual"; one should make the pupils think.

The teacher brings out the items, one by one, after the story has been told. The pupils are asked to write what part each item *may* have played in the story, being careful to stay within its bounds. The integrity of the story must be respected.

• The second form of this activity involves the pupils putting items in a pillowcase. They decide what three items a character may have kept to remind them of the events which took place and their significance. In each case, the pupils have to explain in writing why they think the character kept that particular item. Before doing this latter activity pupils need to see some mementoes to understand the sort of things people keep: a pressed flower, a lock of hair, a baby bootie, holiday souvenirs, and suchlike.

Biblical application

If a teacher uses the example of the good Samaritan, s/he might place in a sack a bandage, a coin and an envelope with a blank piece of paper in it. The teacher brings out the bandage and asks what part it might have played in the story. Allow the pupils to use their imaginations, but they must keep within the bounds of the story. The coin would follow, and, lastly, the letter. Who would have written it? What is it about? To whom was it written? It might have been a thank you letter from the injured man to the Samaritan or a letter to the Council complaining about the dangers of the road! There are many possibilities. The letter gives the pupils scope to explore the meaning of the story.

For the story of Naaman, the teacher could have a phial of water, some soil and a map in the pillowcase. This story can initiate a discussion on God being everywhere. Naaman thought of him as a local god: as if a map could be divided up with different gods ruling each part.

The second form of this activity, in which the pupils select the mementoes a character keeps, works well on the Christmas story (Matthew 1.18–25; 2.1–12; Luke 2.1–20). Tell the pupils the story of Christmas: ask them what three items Mary might have kept and why. What might the shepherds have kept?

Recipes

Ruth and Naomi: Ruth 1.1–22
David and Jonathan: 1 Samuel 18.1–4; 19.4–7; 21.1–42
Love: 1 Corinthians 13

Description of the activity

A recipe is a list of ingredients which, put together in a particular way, in specified proportions, create a cake or some other dish. The format of the recipe can be used in RE using abstract ingredients such as patience and kindness. Go through several recipes with the pupils, listing terms such as:

stir	add a pinch	pour
beat	spoonful	bake
add	gram	decorate
whisk	a cup of	ice
cream	a few drops	serve
fold	sprinkle	leave to rise or cool
rub	scatter	prove

Recipes for teachers, good friends, and whatever you want to make can be written using abstract ingredients such as patience and a sense of humour.

An example

Love

100g of patience
50g of kindness
175g of humility
250g of caring
175g of endurance

200g of faith
100g of truth
50g of sympathy
50g of help

Take humility, whisk until creamy, and knead in patience. Dice kindness, add to humility, and stir. Add endurance to the mixture and beat in hope. Slice truth, rub until it forms breadcrumbs and tip it into the mixture. Add caring. Bake for as long as it takes or until proven. Ice it with sympathy and help. Decorate with faith.

A group of Year 5 and Year 6 pupils, Stevenson Junior School, Stapleford

Biblical application

A recipe for love can be written after exploring 1 Corinthians 13. Pupils should look through the passage listing all the ingredients that make up love: kindness, long-suffering, and the others. They should then put these together in the recipe format. The meaning of the various virtues can be discussed while creating the recipe. It is in this informal discussion that much of the RE happens. In the case of 1 Corinthians, some of the negative statements ("is not proud") have to be changed into positive virtues (humility) to make this form work. The proportions of each ingredient can be listed like a recipe, the proportional size and importance of each quality being discussed beforehand.

Pupils can create a recipe for a friend, and then look at stories of friendship such as that of David and Jonathan, or of Ruth and Naomi.

A recipe for a teacher can be designed, which can be followed by research on Jesus the teacher.

Reviews

Samuel hears God: 1 Samuel 3.1—4.21
The unforgiving servant: Matthew 18.21–35
The lost sheep: Luke 15.1–7; Matthew 18.10–14

Description of the activity

Read a book to the pupils or an extract from a book and then read them a review of it. If possible, use several reviews if you can obtain them. Local libraries often have reviews of books which can be obtained on request. Pupils should note the type of things a reviewer comments on. They can then write their own review on a book or story.

An example

Wonderful Earth
by N Butterworth and M Inkpen (Hunt Thorpe, 1990)

I like this book because I like reading books with pictures in it. The book also told me how the world began and it is very interesting. I think this book is great. It also shows animals you have never seen before and they have got strange names like football fish and the weedy seadragon. On one page it is cut in half and you make animals into other animals. The whole book is about how God made the world. I think it is brilliant!

Claire Lowther, Year 4, St John's Church of England School, Stapleford

Biblical application

Often biblical stories are marketed as separate story books rather than as a complete Bible. The choice of biblical stories will depend on what is available to the teacher. Pupils should have access to a wide variety of biblical stories in individual book format. After choosing a particular book and reading it, they can write their own review commenting not only on the format and illustrations, but also on whether the author has managed to communicate the content and meaning of the story.

Diary

Jacob meets Rachel: Genesis 29.9–30
The widow's offering: Mark 12.41–44; Luke 21.1–4
The entry into Jerusalem: Matthew 21.1–11; Mark 11.1–11; Luke 19.28–44; John 12.12–19

Description of the activity

This activity involves writing in role in order to develop the pupils' imagination and their awareness of others. They write as one character who keeps a diary as a record of events, reflecting their own perspective on those happenings. The diary should include reflection on meaning and significance: it should be more than a factual account. The diary format can be used over a period of time, recording changing events and perceptions. Before starting this activity, pupils should hear extracts from various diaries: Anne Frank, Samuel Pepys, Adrian Mole, for example, in order to experience the range of the form.

An example

Diary of the widow

18th May

I am a poor widow. I only have a few pence to live on. I am thin and tired because I can't afford to eat much. Every Sunday, I go to church, and drop my offering of money into the box. I don't look forward to it because the rich people always put in far more than me. Today when I went to the Temple, I dropped my offering of two small copper coins into the box. The person after me was a rich man and he put 13 large gold coins into the box. I felt ashamed at the tiny amount I had put in but it was all I had. The rich man looked at me in disgust. He said I was a disgrace and I should have put more money in the box. By this time I was feeling very low and downhearted. Just then Jesus came up to me and said, "Why did you feel so ashamed at giving your offering?" I told Jesus I felt ashamed because the rich man gave far more money than I did, I only put two small copper coins into the offering box. "Ah," said Jesus, "I understand, but you actually gave more than the rich man because he only gave a tiny fraction of his wealth, you gave all you had." I suddenly realised that Jesus was right and I should have been happy at giving what I had.

Frances Yuxley, Year 6, Lantern Lane Primary School, East Leake, Loughborough

Biblical application

This activity works for most biblical stories. It works particularly well when there are a number of characters involved as in the stories of the entry into Jerusalem, and Rachel and Jacob. A group can write diary entries for different characters describing the same event. Pupils can be given a page which is laid out as a "day a page" type diary which can be created on the computer. Pupils write either as the person who experienced the events recorded, or as a witness of those events.

Secret files

Jesus the child: Luke 2.40–52

Jesus the friend: Matthew 19.13–15; Luke 19.1–10

Jesus the teacher: John 10.1–21

Jesus the miracle worker: Luke 13.10–17

Jesus the storyteller: Matthew 25.31–46

Description of the activity

The secret file is a collection of pieces of information about an individual or organization. This activity allows pupils – in the role of secret agents, reporters or police – to collect a large amount of data on a person's character, occupation, likes, dislikes, motives, and so on. The file can be stored on computer or in a folder and be in the form of a number of reports. The activity can be done as part of role play or solely as a writing activity.

Each "agent" or reporter is given a task, to investigate a particular biblical incident, person or story. The agent works with a group on their task, and the group spends time investigating the incident and writing the report. The investigation involves reading the stories and writing what they can find out about the character under investigation. They can write an account of the story or imaginary interviews with the characters.

When the reports are complete, the agents can be summoned to a meeting. They deliver their reports, and the leader, editor, Chief of Police decides what to do next.

It is essential that pupils are given a sheet containing all the references and sources of information they need or the teacher will be bombarded for information. In the example below, the information gathered was used to form part of a court case against Jesus.

Examples

Case for the prosecution

He offended the religious leaders because he forgave sins and they said only God could do that. He offended them because he said they made a show of their religion with their long prayers. They said he should not heal on the Sabbath, as it was a day of rest. He mixed with beggars, the poor, tax collectors, lepers, and prostitutes. He turned the market traders out of the Temple because he said they had turned it into a robbers' cave, so the religious leaders lost money.

Case for the defence

He healed lepers, mad people, and the blind. He took care of those considered to be blotted out by God. He ate at the home of a tax collector. He taught people about God. He wouldn't lead an army against Rome, he was peaceful. He never used miracles for himself. He didn't resist when cruelly treated, he said, "Live by the sword, die by the sword."

Rebecca Birch, Year 9, Nottingham High School for Girls

Top Secret File on Jesus bar Joseph

What evidence is there?
Some Roman writers mentioned Jesus, such as Tacitus, a Roman historian. He wrote at the end of the first century AD and early in the second century. When he was writing about the lives of previous Emperors, he mentioned the Christians. "They got their name from Christ, who was executed by the Romans led by Pontius Pilate in the reign of Tiberius."

Tacitus was a non-Christian writer and if Jesus had been a myth, intelligent writers like him and others such as Josephus (a Jewish historian) and Pliny, a Roman writer, would have been quick to point this out.

There is also evidence from Christian writers of the Gospels for although they only describe the actual life of Jesus and not his person, they were written fairly near the time Jesus lived and are therefore primary sources. These are the dates approximately that the gospels were written.
Mark AD65–70, Matthew AD85, Luke AD80–90, John AD100

Alina Myszka, Year 9, Nottingham High School for Girls

Biblical application

The secret file can be used for studying characters in greater depth, allowing pupils to explore the person's character and motives as well as their work. Jesus, Moses, Paul, and Simon Peter are good candidates for such a file, as there are a number of stories concerning them which give the pupils enough information to create a file. Only a few stories are given here.

The context could be an emergency meeting of the Jewish leaders to discuss Jesus who seems to have emerged as a popular preacher. Each agent and their group studies a different story about Jesus, exploring a different aspect. The report is a group effort involving discussion, research, and, if possible, typing the report on the computer. Later, the agents meet to submit their reports and to decide what must be done.

This particular example involves the use of role play, details of which can be found on pages 83–86, *Story and Drama*, but the activity can be done without role play.

Personal passports

Samuel: 1 Samuel 1.1—2.11; 2.18–21; 3.1–21
David: 1 Samuel 16.1–13
John the Baptist: Luke 1.57–66; Matthew 3.1–12

Description of the activity
The "personal passport" gives pupils a brief introduction to a character and allows them to select small amounts of information giving a thumbnail sketch. Pupils will need to design a passport for this and decide what information is important. (This will be different from a conventional passport form). This is a short form of the "Secret files" activity on page 61.

The amount of information should be small and should be contained in the one or two stories the teacher gives the pupils, otherwise the teacher will be constantly having to supply information.

Examples

Samuel's passport

Name: Samuel

Parents: Elkanah and Hannah

Place of birth: Ramah

Occupation: Worshipping the Lord

Home: Shiloh

Main Interests: Finding out about God

Other relevant information: Very religious

Catherine Wright, Year 7, Brambletye Middle School, Surrey

Jesus' passport

Name: Jesus-bar-Joseph

Next of kin: Father, Joseph

Family connections: Brother, James

Date of birth: 4 BC

Place of birth: Bethlehem

Occupation: Carpenter

Address: Nazareth

Marital status: Single

Children: None

Close friends: Simon Peter, James (son of Zebedee), John (son of Zebedee), Andrew, Philip, Bartholomew, Matthew, Thomas, James (son of Alphaeus), Thaddaeus, Simon the Patriot, Judas Iscariot

Description: He would probably have had black shoulder-length hair and an Arabic looking skin as he was born in the East.

Alina Myszka, Year 9, Nottingham High School for Girls

Biblical application

The passport form can be a quick introduction to biblical characters such as John the Baptist, David, the disciples, the prophets, or Jesus himself. It is only an introduction to a character. Sometimes a fuller passport can be created after a longer period of research, as in the second example.

Other activities would be needed to explore meaning. Some aspects of significance can be added under the section "Other relevant information".

Inside, outside

The stilling of the storm: Matthew 8.23–37; Mark 4.35–41; Luke 8.22–25
Jeremiah in the pit: Jeremiah 38.1–28
Elijah and the still, small voice: 1 Kings 19.1–18

Description of the activity

This is a technique used in television and literature. It comes in two forms.

- Television often moves from what is happening inside a building to what is happening outside. In a film, the scene flashes from what is going on inside a house (car, boat, and so on) to what is happening outside.
- In literature, the reader is taken from what is happening inside a character, in their thoughts and feelings, to what is happening outside.

Pupils can use either form of this activity when exploring a story, moving from an internal location to an external one, or moving from what a character is thinking and feeling to events going on around them. The writing should alternate: one sentence on what is happening inside, one sentence on external events. To help pupils it can be arranged as a grid. It can be rearranged afterwards if desired.

Events outside	Events inside

or

Events outside	Feelings and thoughts

An example

The stilling of the storm

Note: The lines in bold are the thoughts of the disciples.

Jesus: "Disciples, we shall go to the other side of the lake by boat."

It should be nice and calm.

A disciple: "Look there are many boats already there."

I am surprised that there are lots of boats.

The waves begin to spill over the boat.

Disciple: "Jesus is sleeping through this."

This is getting really scary, we could die.

Disciple: "Jesus, don't you care about us?"

Jesus doesn't care about us. I don't want to die.

Jesus: "Wind, be quiet, be still."

Wow, the wind and waves obey him. Who is he?

Year 8 pupils, Bishop Ramsey Church of England School, Ruislip

Biblical application

This can be used on most stories. The first form obviously needs a story which has a location which can change. The second activity allows pupils to explore the emotions of the characters involved, and the impact of events on people. In the case of the stilling of the storm, the location should move from what is happening inside the boat to what is happening outside it.

If the second form is used, the writing should alternate between what the people are thinking and feeling and external events. In the case of Jeremiah it can move from inside the pit to outside, or inside Jeremiah's head to the conditions of the pit. In the story of Elijah, the writing moves from what is happening inside Elijah to what is going on outside.

Keyhole

The Last Supper: Matthew 26.17–35; Mark 14.12–31; Luke 22.7–38; John 13
Samuel hears God: 1 Samuel 3
The lost coin: Luke 15.8–10

Description of the activity

For this activity, a character looks through a hole, a window, a keyhole, or some type of aperture into the story. It is written as if by an outsider looking in and describing what is happening and trying to make sense of it. Because the observer is not part of the story, they are free to comment, ask questions, and so on. Tell the pupils a suitable story and ask them to imagine looking through a keyhole or knot hole in a wooden wall. Ask them to imagine that the story they have just heard is happening inside the room. They should then describe what they see as if they are a person or animal peeping through a window, keyhole, or similar aperture. If an animal is used this activity is similar to "What the donkey saw" on page 42. The use of the keyhole narrows the focus, it is like masking a painting and only letting a child see a small section. The person/animal peeping through the keyhole can often describe only a section of the story, though some children want to tell the whole story, as in the example.

An example

The call of Samuel
by a Desert Squirrel

I pulled off a roof piece, looking for dry material, and a boy was there, lying wrapped in a goatskin blanket. I pulled up another roof piece a few yards away. A man. A man, lying asleep. Then, suddenly, I heard a movement. The boy was sitting up in bed. He got up and went into the old man's room. I moved rooms to see what happened.

"What's wrong, Samuel?" asked the man.
"You called me, Eli?" answered Samuel.
"No, Samuel, no. Go back to bed."
I settled down in the rafters to sleep.

I woke up at 1:00 am to the sound of the squeaky door. In came Samuel. "Yes, master?" he said.

"Go back to bed! I never called you" came the cross answer.

I puzzled myself to sleep.

Again, the door creaked.

"Eli, you did call me, didn't you?"

"No! But next time you hear something, don't run in here. Stay where you are and say, 'Speak Lord, your servant is listening.' Now go to bed!"

I didn't go to sleep. I stayed awake to watch Samuel. I saw him move. "Speak Lord, your, gulp, servant is listening," the boy trembled.

All I heard was, "Yes," "Oh my," "Me" and "Gulp."

Confused, I got some sleep.

Next morning, Eli said to Samuel, "What did God say?" Samuel hesitated. "Come on," said Eli.

"He said that... that... that I was going to be the... the next priest!"

"You did right to tell me," said Eli.

Lucy Parkinson, Year 4, Brennands Endowed Church of England School, Slaidburn

Biblical application

This technique can be used on stories that take place inside a building of some sort. Another alternative is for the character to look from behind a rock or similar object which allows a greater choice of stories. It could be a child who looks through a knot hole in the wood of the door in the upper room where the Last Supper took place. A mouse could be peeping through a hole in the Temple wall in the story of Samuel. A neighbour could stare through the window of the house of the woman who lost her coin.

Sequencing

Daniel and the lions: Daniel 6.1–28
The parable of the talents: Matthew 25.14–30
Zacchaeus: Luke 19.1–27

Description of the activity

Sequencing helps pupils to organize material in the correct order. They can be given a story which has been jumbled by the teacher. This can be done either before or after the correct sequence of the story has been told, depending on the age of the pupils. The story can be jumbled on the computer and pupils can order it correctly using cut and paste. An alternative is to give them a jumbled version on paper and ask them to cut up the text and attempt to paste it together in the correct order, or to rewrite it, or to number the sentences correctly. This is one way of helping pupils master content.

An example

Paul at Ephesus: Acts 19.23–41

Jumbled example

Paul told many people about Jesus and many people believed what he said. Paul went to Ephesus. The crowd was angry. Everyone shouted, "Great is Artemis of the Ephesians." A man named Demetrius sold silver statues of the goddess Artemis. He made a lot of money from this. Paul went to another town. Demetrius told everyone that people would stop worshipping Artemis because they believed in Jesus. A man quietened everyone down so that Paul was not killed.

Hilltop Junior School, Derby

Sequenced version

Paul went to Ephesus. Paul told many people about Jesus, and many people believed what he said. A man named Demetrius sold silver statues of the goddess Artemis, he made a lot of money from this. Demetrius told everyone that people would stop worshipping Artemis because they believed in Jesus. The crowd was angry. Everyone shouted, "Great is Artemis of the Ephesians." A man quietened everyone down so that Paul was not killed. Paul went to another town.

Alan Byrne, Year 3, Hilltop Junior School, Derby

Biblical application

For this technique, a story is needed of suitable length and with a strong story line such as Daniel, a parable, or a story such as Zacchaeus. The example given has the story already jumbled. This can be photocopied and given to the pupils to put in the correct order. Pupils can discuss the order the events should take and this can lead to exploring the meaning of those events. In the story of Paul at Ephesus would the idol makers have been angry before or after Paul had preached? Why?

The story can be typed into the computer and pupils can use cut and paste to put it in the right sequence.

Personality sketch

Jacob: Genesis 25.27–34; 27.1–29
Esther: The Book of Esther
The woman who washed Jesus' feet: Luke 7.36–50

Description of the activity

A sketch tries not only to capture a likeness of the person but also to capture something of their personality. A sketch has few lines and is not detailed in the same way that a painting is. A personality sketch should do the same. Pupils can write sketches of particular characters, trying to express something of their personality in under 50 words. As a practice exercise, ask the pupils to list a set number of adjectives to describe a chosen character's personality. These can then be turned into a sketch. Sketches can be created for a number of characters within a story so that a range of people can be seen at a glance.

Examples

Personality sketches of Esther

A kind, loyal person. She helps people. She is brave and thoughtful. No matter who you are she will help you. If you were lonely she would be your friend.

Mark Allum, Year 5

She was loyal, caring, and kind. She was brave enough to speak up and save her people from being killed. She was trustworthy and loving and wasn't easily frightened.

Rebecca Glenn, Year 6, Pupils of Stevenson Junior School, Stapleford

Biblical application

After reading or listening to a Bible story, pupils can list adjectives to describe various characters within the story and discuss what those words mean. The words become part of the character sketch. It is in discussion that much RE happens. The teacher can deepen the discussion by following up the pupil's suggestions, as in this example:

Simon Pratt: Esther was loyal to her religion.

Teacher: In what way was Esther loyal to her faith? What about the time when she kept quiet about being Jewish?

Stories such as Esther are long and will need retelling in the teacher's own words.

Wordsearches and crosswords

The Ten Commandments: Deuteronomy 5.6–21
The Pharisee and the tax collector: Luke 18.9–14
The parable of the sower: Matthew: 13.1–23; Mark 4.1–20; Luke 8.4–15

Description of the activity

These two techniques are good for mastering content. In a wordsearch, the pupils pick out words important to the story and hide them among a number of letters on a square as in the example. Another pupil then has to find them, using a list provided. Emphasis on meaning can be created by asking pupils to list what they consider the ten most significant words in the story – significant people, important places, and important words which convey meaning or feelings. In each case, the pupils should be able to justify their choice. Clues can be written for wordsearches which help bring out meaning as well as content.

Crosswords can be constructed in a similar way, but in this case the pupil has to supply the word rather than find it. The clues can be formed as for the wordsearch.

The Pharisee and the tax collector

(1) The religious leader was called a ...

(2) The tax-collector felt ...

(3) A word which would describe the attitude of the Pharisee ...

(4) The two men prayed in the ...

An example

R	W	H	O	L	E	W	O	R	L	D	S	E	N
I	E	C	L	O	U	D	E	N	E	V	A	E	H
S	Z	G	E	Z	E	B	B	H	V	S	I	R	E
E	I	R	W	P	J	E	R	U	S	A	L	E	M
N	T	F	I	R	E	J	A	G	A	H	C	S	A
S	P	H	N	A	S	F	V	H	O	I	H	U	L
W	A	O	D	Y	U	I	E	I	R	D	R	R	F
E	B	L	M	A	S	P	I	R	I	T	I	R	V
N	T	Y	D	L	C	Z	J	K	G	K	S	E	W
D	S	N	P	E	N	T	E	C	O	S	T	C	X
O	I	O	L	A	V	I	T	S	E	F	I	T	V
O	R	N	O	I	S	N	E	C	S	A	A	I	Z
G	H	W	O	N	D	E	R	F	U	L	N	O	Y
P	C	R	S	T	U	E	F	I	L	W	E	N	Q

Wind
Fire
Jesus
Jerusalem
Resurrection
God
Spirit
Holy
Brave
Good news
Ascension
Pentecost

Whole world
New life
Heaven
Cloud
Flame
Christian
Christ
Wonderful
Risen
Festival
Pray
Baptize

Kajal Kothari, Year 6, Dovelands Junior School, Leicester

Biblical application

In the stories of the Pharisee and the tax collector, of the sower, and of the Ten Commandments, the pupils should read one story and decide on important places, people, and meaning. They should also note the emotions and attitudes of the characters. Clues should be designed, by groups of pupils, which reflect all these parts of the story.

At the end of the exercise, groups can swap crosswords or wordsearches.

Different ways of looking

Jesus described from many people's perspectives:

Mary: Jesus the child lost in the Temple: Luke 2.40–50
Pilate: Jesus the criminal: John 18.28—19.6
Martha and Mary: Jesus the friend: Luke 10.38–42
Jairus' daughter: Jesus the miracle worker: Matthew 9.18–26
A member of the crowd: Jesus the storyteller and teacher: Matthew 18.21–35

Description of the activity

This technique looks at a person or event from many different angles. A person can play many roles, and be seen differently by a variety of people. Events, too, cause different reactions: the resurrection was not an occasion for joy for the Roman and Jewish authorities!

Introduce the pupils to this technique by talking about the way a person fulfils different roles. We are daughter, friend, pupil, employee, depending on who we are relating to. Look at a character from a story and write about the way they are viewed by other characters.

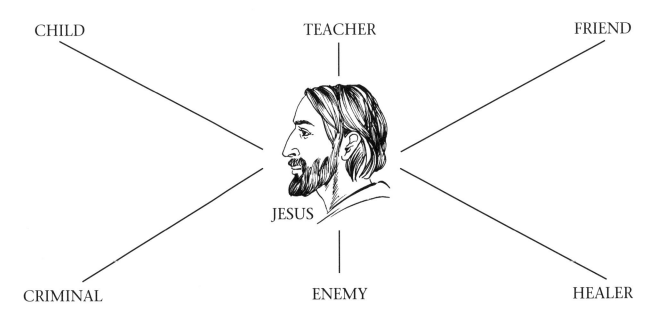

CHILD   TEACHER   FRIEND

CRIMINAL   ENEMY   HEALER

74

An example

Joseph

Joseph
My name is Joseph. I'm the youngest son of Jacob and he loves me more than he loves all my brothers put together. That's why he gave me this wonderful coat. I can interpret dreams and I know that one day all my brothers will bow down to me.

Jacob
I am Jacob, Joseph's father. He's a good kid. That's why I bought him a colourful coat. I couldn't afford to get one for all my boys but Joseph deserved it more than they did. I don't think they really mind because he is the youngest after all.

The brothers
Joseph, our brother, has all the luck, it really isn't fair. He really thinks that he is best. We should teach him a lesson. I know, we'll kill him. Serve him right. He's a pompous boy, our brother is.

Judah
Hang on a sec, you can't do that. Joseph is our brother. Why don't you sell him to those traders. We'll just tell father he's dead.

Potiphar

I am Potiphar, Joseph works for me. He works hard and that's all that matters.

Potiphar's wife

I hate Joseph. I want him out. I wish he didn't work for my husband Potiphar. I'll make up some story about the man and Joseph will end up in jail.

Butler

I am the butler and I had a dream. Joseph told me that I would be freed and I was.

Baker

Alas, if only I had been so lucky. Joseph told me that I would be hung and I was.

Pharoah

I am the Pharoah and I had a dream. Nobody knew what it meant. Joseph stepped in and told me of the famine. Because of him we now have food.

Carmen Whelas, Year 7, Nottingham High School for Girls

Biblical application

Many people or stories of the Bible can be explored using this technique. Easter can be a sad story or a joyful one: it depends what moment you choose, or which character you are. Jesus can be a miracle worker or a rabble rouser, depending on your point of view. Short descriptions, in poetry or prose, can be written from different points of view. For example, a piece entitled "Six ways of looking at Jesus" could contain one section written by someone in the role of Mary, another section written in the role of Pilate, and so on.

Journeys

The wandering in the wilderness: Exodus 13.17—14.31 (Red Sea)

Exodus 16.1–36 (manna and quail)

Exodus 19.1—20.21 (Ten Commandments)

Paul's journey to Rome and shipwreck: Acts 27

Description of the activity

This activity involves writing about a journey and the events which happened, or may have happened, during its course. Once the pupils have heard the story, they write about different events which occurred. These events can be shared out across a class or group, or can be tackled over a period of time. A large sheet of frieze paper could be rolled along a wall, and the course of the journey drawn on it. Pupil's work, about events which happened along the way, can be attached to the journey frieze. Artwork may be added.

If it is a journey about which little is known, they can write what the people may have said to each other, as long as pupils stay within the bounds of the story.

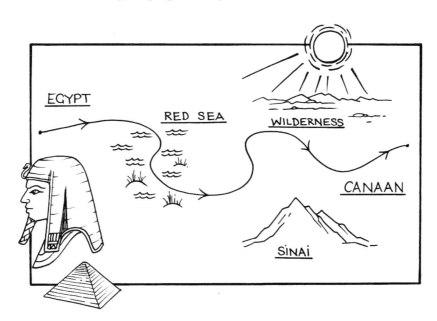

Biblical application

Any story involving a journey can be used for this activity. Jesus' ministry, Jonah, Paul, Abraham, the wandering in the wilderness, or the flight into Egypt by Mary and Joseph would all be suitable stories. Stories such as the Good Samaritan can also be used, with imaginative writing from the point of view of different characters displayed along the journey line from Jericho to Jerusalem.

In the case of the flight into Egypt, we know little of what happened on the way, so pupils would have to imagine what Joseph and Mary may have encountered and what they said to each other. The thoughts of the characters as they travel and the way in which they react to events can help bring out meaning.

POETRY

INTRODUCTION

Background

The Bible is full of poetry, particularly the Old Testament. It is not only the writers of the Psalms who use poetry. Mary speaks poetically in her song of praise (Luke 1.46–55), Moses and Deborah in their songs of triumph (Judges 5 and Deuteronomy 32). David's lament over Jonathan (2 Samuel 1.17–27) is in the form of a poem, as are many of the prophets' declarations. The Song of Songs, a book of the Old Testament, is a long love poem:

> How beautiful you are, my love!
> How your eyes shine with love behind your
>   veil.
> Your hair dances, like a flock of goats
> bounding down the hills of Gilead.
> Your teeth are as white as sheep
> that have just been shorn and washed.
> Not one of them is missing;
> they are all perfectly matched.
> Your lips are like a scarlet ribbon;
> how lovely they are when you speak.
>
> Like a lily among thorns
> is my darling among women.

Song of Songs 4.1–3; 2.2

In love, grief, worship, and joy, the characters of the Bible express themselves in poetry. Christianity, too, has a long history of believers who expressed their faith in this form, from the great Saxon poems to Milton's *Paradise Lost,* from William Langland's *Piers Plowman* to Charles Causley's *Ballad of the Bread Man.* Many ordinary Christians, whose names never reach the public, express their own faith in poetry as part of their worship.

If the sacred book of the Christians contains large amounts of poetry, it follows that poetry is suited to expressing the Christian faith and therefore has a role to play in RE where that faith is explored. In the classroom, however, the role of poetry in RE varies. For some it will be a means of expressing a personal faith. For others it will be a way of understanding what is important to someone else.

Poetry needs no defending as part of the school curriculum, but it is not always included as a means of learning and expression in Religious Education. Poetry is, however, an ideal way to explore the Bible.

- Poetry is powerful. It often goes straight to the emotions and sums up, by its unusual use of words, thoughts and feelings which people struggle to express.
- Poetry can challenge, stimulate, provoke discussion and present an unusual angle on a subject.
- Poetry is a vehicle for expressing important and difficult ideas.
- The images poetry uses help pupils grasp the way in which language is used in the Bible. The Bible is rich in images conveyed by metaphor and simile.
- Writing poetry not only helps pupils express their own thoughts and feelings, but also

enables them to explore a biblical character's perspective.

• Poetry allows pupils to engage with the Bible at a level which is more than just intellectual. This is both an advantage and a difficulty. There are some techniques which are too "affective" to use with certain RE content (for example, the crucifixion). Teachers need to select subjects for poetry appropriately.

Poetry raises the awareness of pupils, which is essential in RE. The creative process involved in writing or in listening to poetry also encourages response, decision making, and analysis, all vital elements in RE.

> For lo, the winter is past,
> the rain is over and gone ...
> the time of singing has come,
> and the voice of the turtledove is heard in our
>   land.

Song of Songs 2.11–12 (RSV)

Resources

Books

General technique

BP Teacher's Poetry Resources File for Primary Schools (The Poetry Society, 1992)

BP Teacher's Poetry Resources File for Secondary Schools (The Poetry Society, 1992)

Paths into Poetry by J Collie and G Porter Laddousse (OUP, 1992)

Bright Ideas Poetry by I Souter (Scholastic, 1993)

Poetry for Life by L Hall (Cassell, 1989)

The Essential Guide to Poetry by D Orme (Folens, 1992)

The Poetry Processor volumes 1,2, and 3 by P Higgins (Simon & Schuster, 1989, 1990, 1991)

Meet and Write volumes 1,2, and 3 by A and S Brownjohn (Hodder & Stoughton, 1987, 1988)

Does it Have to Rhyme? by S Brownjohn (Hodder & Stoughton, 1991)

What Rhymes with Secret? by S Brownjohn (Hodder & Stoughton, 1991)

The Ability to Name Cats by S Brownjohn (Hodder & Stoughton, 1989)

Catapults and Kingfishers by P Corbett and B Moses (OUP, 1987)

Word Games by S Brownjohn and J Whitaker (Hodder & Stoughton, 1987)

More Word Games by S Brownjohn and J Whitaker (Hodder & Stoughton, 1988)

Presenting Poetry volumes 1,2,3, and 4 by P McCall and S Palmer (Oliver & Boyd, 1986)

Writing Poems by M Harrison and C Stuart-Clark (OUP, 1987)

Brain Waves Poetry by C Webster (Folens, 1990) (junior)

How to be Brilliant at Writing Poetry by I Yates (Brilliant Publications, 1993)

The Thirteen Secrets of Poetry by A Mitchell (Simon & Schuster, 1993)

Poems 7–11 (Ideas Bank Series) by R Brown (Folens, 1993)

Anthologies of Christian poems

Secondary to adult

The Oxford Book of Christmas Poetry compiled by
     M Harrison and C Stuart-Clark (OUP, 1991)
A Touch of Flame by J Robertson (Lion, 1989)
Faith in Her Words by V Zundel (Lion, 1991)
The Lion Book of Christian Poetry compiled by
     P Alexander (Lion, 1981)
The Sun, Dancing edited by C Causley (Kestrel,
     1982)
Words for Easter edited by P Egan (CHP, 1990)
Pocket Christmas by N and H Whitehead (Church
     House Publishing/National Society, 1995)
The Lion Christian Poetry Collection edited by
     M Batchelor (Lion, 1995)

Junior

Whispering in God's Ear compiled by A MacDonald
     (Lion, 1994)
A Single Star compiled by D Davis (Puffin, 1976)
The Oxford Book of Christmas Poems edited by
     M Harrison and C Stuart-Clarke (OUP, 1991)
Bright Star Shining edited by M Harrison and
     C Stuart-Clark (OUP, 1993)
Words for Easter edited by P Egan (Church House
     Publishing, 1990) (top junior)
Pocket Christmas by N and H Whitehead (Church
     House Publishing/National Society, 1995)
Magic Mirror and Midnight Forest. This is a double
     volume by Judith Nicolls (Faber and Faber,
     1985). Although a general collection of her
     poems, it contains a number of biblical items.

Poetry in the Bible

The majority of the Bible is presented as prose, but much of it may in fact be poetry. Working out what is poetry and what isn't is not easy, as Hebrew poetry does not rhyme, and many of the features which mark out Hebrew poetry – such as stress, alliteration and gender – are lost in translation. There are also poems in the New Testament, the Hebrew forms being reflected in the Greek of the New Testament. The "Magnificat" (Luke 1.46–55) is an example of this, and Hebrew poetry may be behind great passages such as 1 Corinthians 13, Paul's description of love. The New Testament contains echoes of Greek poetry such as 1 Corinthians 15.33, which is from a poem by the Greek poet Menander, but the chief poetic influence is the Old Testament.

Some features of biblical poetry are indicated overleaf; when looking up these references in the Bible it may be helpful to use a Revised Standard Version as well as the Good News version as the poetry is not always preserved in the modern translations.

Features of Hebrew poetry

Parallelism

This is usually considered to be the outstanding feature of Hebrew poetry, but there are many different types, some of which are extremely complicated. This section will only deal with three simple forms.

Basic parallelism

Here a thought is expressed twice (or more) in different terms, one line paralleling the other in thought. Sometimes the second line expresses exactly the same thought, sometimes it expands it, sometimes it highlights the thought by expressing its opposite.

Example:

A child is born to us!

A son is given to us!

Isaiah 9.6

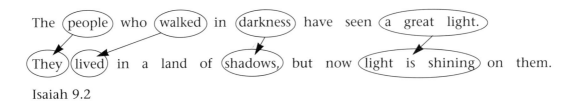

The people who walked in darkness have seen a great light.
They lived in a land of shadows, but now light is shining on them.

Isaiah 9.2

My heart praises the Lord,
my soul is glad because of God my Saviour.

Luke 1.46–47

A parallel expressed in opposites:

> He has filled the hungry with good things,
> and sent the rich away with empty hands.

Luke 1.52–53

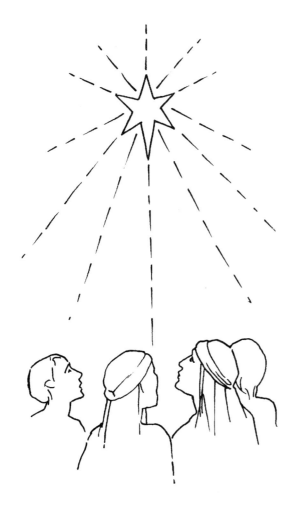

"Chi" parallelism

Chi is the Greek letter which is written like this X.

Chi parallelism sometimes forms this shape. In some forms of this type of parallelism the order of the components of the lines is completely reversed.

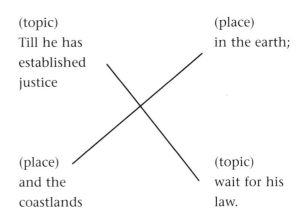

(topic)
Till he has established justice

(place)
in the earth;

(place)
and the coastlands

(topic)
wait for his law.

Isaiah 42.4 (RSV); see also Isaiah 22.22 and Philippians 3.7–8

Staircase parallelism

In this form of parallelism, the same idea is expressed several times with a repeating phrase but each time something extra is added to build up the meaning or flesh out the description.

> It is not for kings, O Lemuel,
> It is not for kings to drink wine,
> or for rulers to desire strong drink.

Proverbs 31.4 (RSV); see also Psalm 29.1

The parallel structure of Hebrew poetry, by its very nature, concentrates on ideas and meaning. The same idea may be expressed in three different ways. This form makes it an ideal vehicle for the communication of meaning when pupils write their own religious poetry using these structures. The poems pupils write might be from the point of view of a particular biblical character, or, if appropriate, the pupils can use this form for expressing their own thoughts.

Choruses, refrains and repeating lines.

Choruses, refrains and repeating lines are often used in Hebrew poetry. Psalm 136 has the line "His love is eternal" repeated after every line. In Amos 1 and 2 the line "for three sins ... and for four" is repeated eight times.

> Give thanks to the LORD, because he is good;
> his love is eternal.
> Give thanks to the greatest of all gods;
> his love is eternal.
> Give thanks to the mightiest of all lords;
> his love is eternal.
> He alone performs great miracles;
> his love is eternal.
> By his wisdom he made the heavens;
> his love is eternal;
> he built the earth on the deep waters;
> his love is eternal.
> He made the sun and the moon;
> his love is eternal;
> the sun to rule over the day;
> his love is eternal;
> the moon and the stars to rule over the night;
> his love is eternal.

Psalm 136.1–9

Alphabet poems

Psalm 119 is an alphabet poem which has twenty-two eight-line sections. The initial letters of the first words of each section form the Hebrew alphabet. If you look in a New International Version of the Bible, you will see each section headed by a letter of the Hebrew alphabet.

Section 1 starts with a word beginning with

א – Aleph

Section 2 starts with a word beginning with

ב – Bet

Psalm 119 is particularly clever because every verse *within* a section starts with the same letter of the alphabet. Section 1 has eight lines each beginning with a word starting with Aleph, section 2 has eight lines each beginning with a word starting with Bet.

NOTE: Hebrew poetry is very complicated: this is a simplified account.

Biblical poems

Happy are those who reject the advice of evil
    people,
who do not follow the example of sinners
or join those who have no use for God ...
They are like trees that grow beside a stream,
that bear fruit at the right time,
and whose leaves do not dry up.

Psalm 1.1,3

The Lord is my protector; he is my strong
    fortress.
My God is my protection, and with him I am
    safe.
He protects me like a shield; he defends me and
    keeps me safe.

Psalm 18.2

I am worn out with grief;
every night my bed is damp from my weeping;
my pillow is soaked with tears.

Psalm 6.6

Can you shout orders to the clouds
and make them drench you with rain?
And if you command the lightning to flash,
will it come to you and say, "At your service"?

Job 38.34–35

Holy, holy, holy, is the Lord God Almighty,
who was and is and is to come!

Revelation 4.8 (RSV)

He has brought down mighty kings from their
    thrones,
and lifted up the lowly.
He has filled the hungry with good things,
and sent the rich away with empty hands.

Luke 1.52–53

My teaching will fall like drops of rain
and form on the earth like dew.
My words will fall like showers on young
    plants,
like gentle rain on tender grass.
Deuteronomy 32.2

I am the good shepherd.
As the Father knows me and I know the Father,
in the same way I know my sheep and they
    know me.
John 10.14–15

I am worn out from calling for help, and my
    throat is aching.
I have strained my eyes looking for your help.
Psalm 69.3

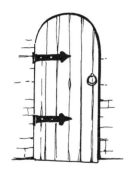

What he opens, no one will shut,
and what he shuts, no one will open.
Isaiah 22.22

Wake up, my soul!
Wake up, my harp and lyre!
I will wake up the sun.
Psalm 57.8

They shall hunger no more, neither shall they
    thirst;
the sun shall not strike them, nor any
    scorching heat.
For the Lamb will be their shepherd
and guide them to springs of
    living water;
and God will wipe away every
    tear from their eyes.
Revelation 7.16–17 (RSV adapted)

The Lord is my shepherd;
I have everything I need.
He lets me rest in fields of
    green grass
and leads me to quiet pools of
    fresh water.
He gives me new strength.
He guides me in the right paths,
as he has promised.
Even if I go through the deepest
    darkness,
I will not be afraid, Lord,
for you are with me.
Your shepherd's rod and staff protect me.
Psalm 23.1–4

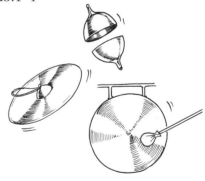

Paul's Hymn of love

If I speak in the tongues of men and of angels,
but have not love,
I am a noisy gong or a clanging cymbal.
And if I have prophetic powers,
and understand all mysteries and all
    knowledge,
and if I have all faith, so as to remove
    mountains,
but have not love,
I am nothing.
If I give away all I have,

and if I deliver my body to be burned,
but have not love,
I gain nothing.
Love is patient and kind;
love is not jealous or boastful;
it is not arrogant or rude.
Love does not insist on its own way;
it is not irritable or resentful;
it does not rejoice at wrong,
but rejoices in the right.
Love bears all things,
believes all things,
hopes all things,
endures all things.

Love never ends;
as for prophecies,
they will pass away;
as for tongues,
they will cease;
as for knowledge,
it will pass away.

For our knowledge is imperfect
and our prophecy is imperfect;
but when the perfect comes,
the imperfect will pass away.

When I was a child,
I spoke like a child,
I thought like a child,
I reasoned like a child;
when I became a man,
I gave up childish ways.
For now we see in a mirror dimly,
but then face to face.
Now I know in part;
then I shall understand fully,
even as I have been fully understood.
So faith, hope, love abide,
these three;
but the greatest of these is love.

1 Corinthians 13 (rearranged as poetry from
the RSV)

Activities based on biblical poetry

All the activities in this section are based on simple Hebrew forms of poetry which are detailed on pages 83–5.

Parallel practice

Ask the pupils to write one statement, for example "I hate rain", and then write the same sentiment in a different way underneath. Give them practice at expressing the same idea in various ways.

I hate the rain,
I'm miserable when it pours down.

These parallels can be two lines or three. One way of doing this is to ask one pupil to write the basic statement; s/he passes it on to the next pupil, who has to express it in different words and then pass it on to a third pupil, who does the same. Once pupils have gained some skill in writing parallels, these can be used on religious subjects. Pupils can use them to write prayers if appropriate, or to write a prayer that a character from a biblical story might have prayed.

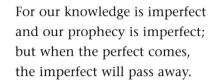

Give praise to the Lord
Shout his glory
Give thanks to the Lord
Cry out his goodness

Jodie Chaplin, Year 5; Ben Brindley, Year 6, Stevenson Junior School, Stapleford.

Guess the parallel

Give the pupils a number of single lines from biblical poems. Each pupil or pair of pupils should have one line. Ask them to think carefully about the meaning of that line and write what they think the next line is, bearing in mind that they are written in parallel.

One way of working out what the parallel might be is to circle the main words of the first line and find alternatives to those words using a junior thesaurus. When this is done, the rest of the line can be filled in.

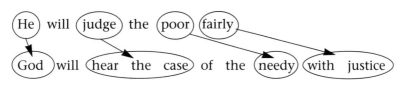

Isaiah 11.4

Examples of first lines are given below (extra examples can be found in the Book of Psalms).

When pupils have written their own second lines, they can look up the original. How close were they? Is the meaning the same?

> Give thanks to the Lord, proclaim his greatness.
> (1 Chronicles 16.8)
>
> Do you find food for lions to eat?
> (Job 38.39)
>
> Happy are those who reject the advice of evil
> people. (Psalm 1.1)
>
> When I look at the sky, which you have made.
> (Psalm 8.3)
>
> No speech or words are used.
> (Psalm 19.3)
>
> I am in trouble, God – listen to my prayer!
> (Psalm 64.1)
>
> They have eyes but they are blind.
> (Isaiah 43.8)
>
> He will judge the poor fairly.
> (Isaiah 11.4)

The parallel matching game

Photocopy the parallel pairs on the next page and glue them to card. Select enough two-line parallels from the list overleaf for each pupil to have one line. Cut the parallels into single lines, muddle them up and give each pupil one line. Some pupils will have a card with a (1) on it, some will have a card marked (2).

Pupils can move around looking at other people's lines in order to find a line which parallels theirs. If a pupil has a card marked (2), they have to find a matching parallel marked (1). As soon as a pair has been found, that pair of pupils sits down. While waiting for the others, they should look at their pair of lines and decide on its meaning.

NOTE: This game is noisy but fun and is best played in the hall or a similar area. A quiet version of the game can be played by creating two lists, side by side, on one sheet of paper. One list contains all the lines labelled (1) in any order. The second list contains all the lines labelled (2) in a different order. Pupils draw coloured lines between the two lists to match up the correct lines.

Suitable verses for the matching parallel game

(1) A child is born to us!

(2) A son is given to us!

(1) How much longer will you forget me Lord?

(2) How much longer will you hide yourself from me?

(1) I will always thank the LORD;

(2) I will never stop praising him.

(1) No speech or words are used,

(2) No sound is heard.

(1) Your constant love is my guide;

(2) Your faithfulness always leads me.

(1) Even if a whole army surrounds me, I will not be afraid;

(2) Even if enemies attack me, I will still trust God.

(1) Hear me, LORD, when I call to you

(2) Be merciful and answer me!

(1) You have given them great joy, Lord;

(2) You have made them happy.

(1) Don't let me bring shame on those who trust in you, Sovereign Lord Almighty

(2) Don't let me bring disgrace to those who worship you, O God of Israel!

(1) The voice of the Lord makes the lightning flash

(2) His voice makes the desert shake.

(1) You have changed my sadness into a joyful dance;

(2) You have taken away my sorrow and surrounded me with joy.

(1) My heart praises the Lord;

(2) My soul is glad because of God my saviour.

(1) I will make a highway across the mountains

(2) And make a road for my people to travel.

(1) The water came over me and choked me;

(2) The sea covered me completely.

(1) The people who walked in darkness have seen a great light.

(2) They lived in a land of shadows, but now light is shining on them.

(1) They will hammer their swords into ploughs

(2) And their spears into pruning knives.

(1) Help us Lord! There is not a good person left.

(2) Honest people can no longer be found.

© 1996 Bible Society. This page may be photocopied for classroom use only.

"Chi" parallels

Repeat the activity on page 88 with the pupils, then ask them to reverse the order of the second line to make it chiastic (like the letter Chi).

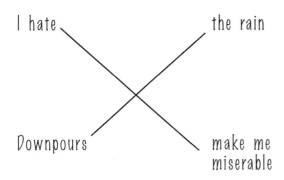

These chiastic parallels can then be used to explore religious subjects, create prayers, etc.

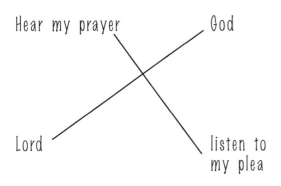

Kylie Brown, Year 6, Stevenson Junior School, Stapleford

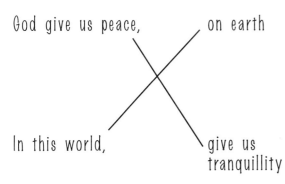

Stacey Harrop, Year 6, Stevenson Junior School, Stapleford

Staircase parallelism

These can be short poems of two or three lines with a repeating phrase. Each line should express the same sentiment, but add to the meaning or description.

> I hate Monday morning
> I hate Monday morning when it's dark and wet
> I hate Monday morning when it's dark, wet, and November.

Once pupils have mastered the basic idea, they can experiment with the form.

The biblical form does not always repeat the phrase every time.

> He lies in wait like a lion in cover;
> he lies in wait to catch the helpless;
> he catches the helpless and drags them off in his net.

Psalm 10.9 (NIV)

Once pupils are used to the form, they can create their own staircases.

> Give thanks to the Lord.
> Give thanks to the Lord for the world.
> Give thanks to the Lord for the world and everything in it.

> Help me God
> Help me God, hear my prayer,
> Help me God, hear my prayer, and come.

Louise Leverton and Sam Sneesby, Year 6, Stevenson Junior School, Stapleford

Alphabet poems

Alphabet poems (non-rhyming) can be created on a number of biblical subjects, such as the things God created. The poems should comment, not just describe. Alphabet poems can be done as a class once an agreed pattern is decided upon, the letters of the alphabet being shared amongst groups.

ABC

> God made:
> The agile ape
> the darting butterfly
> the armoured crab.
> And God saw that it was good.

Images

Look through some of the biblical poems on page 86 and write down some of the images used. For example, God is described as a shepherd in Psalm 23. What meaning is being communicated through the images used?

Metaphors and similes

Choose a biblical poem from page 86 or one from the Book of Psalms, and underline metaphors and similes (page 117). Why does the poet use those particular metaphors and similes? What meaning is being communicated through them?

Looking for parallels

Pupils can try to pick out various types of parallel within biblical poems. How does the use of parallelism help to convey the meaning?

Choruses and Refrains

Read Psalm 69.1–5. Talk with the pupils about its meaning. What would be a suitable chorus or repeating line to add to this psalm? Rewrite the psalm and add the chorus or repeating line at suitable points.

Modern biblical poems

Most of the following poems are based on biblical stories, characters or ideas. The poem "The rich eat three full meals" is a more general poem on peace of mind and enjoying God's world. The poems can just be read or they can be the basis for follow-up work.

My Bath

My bath is the ocean
and I am a continent
with hills and valleys
and earthquakes and storms.
I put the two mountain peaks of my knees
underwater and bring them up again.

Our earth was like that—
great churnings and splashings,
and continents appearing and disappearing.
Only you, O God, know about it all,
and understand and take care
of all creation.

Madeleine L'Engle

Activity
Ask the pupils about things they have made. How do they feel about things they have created? Make a display of items by members of the class. Read the poem "My Bath" and the account of creation in Genesis 1. How does God feel about his creation in the story?

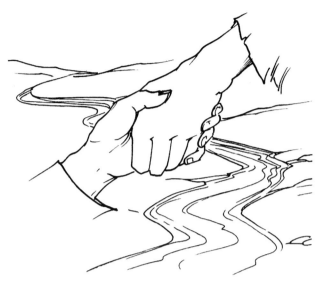

John, John the Baptist

John, John the Baptist
Lived in a desert of stone,
He had no money,
Ate beans and honey,
And he lived quite on his own.

His coat was made of camel,
His belt was made of leather,
And deep in the gleam
Of a twisting stream
He'd stand in every weather.

John, John the Baptist,
Worked without any pay,
But he'd hold your hand
And bring you to land
And wash your fears away.

Charles Causley

Activity
Read the story of John the Baptist (Luke 3) and the poem. What are the "fears" John washes away in this poem? Pupils can draw a large water drop and write within it one "fear" that might have been washed away.

The rich eat three full meals

The rich eat three full meals, the poor two
    small bowls,
But peace is what matters.
Thirsty, I drink sweet plum tea;
Warm, I lie in the shade, in the breeze;
My paintings are mountains and rivers all
    around me,
My damask, embroidered, the grass.
I rest at night, rest easy,
Am awake with the sun
And enjoying Heaven's heaped-up favors.

Nguyen Binh Khiem

Activity

Read the poem carefully. What makes a person rich? What makes someone poor? Is the poet rich or poor? What sort of riches does the poet have? Pupils might like to write about their "riches", the ones that come free with creation.

Christmas is really for the children

Christmas is really
for the children.
Especially for children
who like animals, stables,
stars and babies wrapped
in swaddling clothes.
Then there are wise men,
kings in fine robes,
humble shepherds and a
hint of rich perfume.

Easter is not really
for the children
unless accompanied by
a cream-filled egg.
It has whips, blood, nails,
a spear and allegations
of body snatching.
It involves politics, God
and the sins of the world.
It is not good for people
of a nervous disposition.
They would do better to
think on rabbits, chickens
and the first snowdrop
    of spring.

Or they'd do better to
wait for a re-run of
Christmas without asking
too many questions about
what Jesus did when he grew up
or whether there's any connection.

Steve Turner

Activity

The nativity story is often dismissed as something for younger children. Look closely at the story (Matthew 1.18—2.18). If a realistic film were made of this story, what rating would you give it?

Jonah

Jonah was a later one
among God's prophets,
not one to be sat upon,
didn't do as asked;
you could even say, alas,
he was rather like a
naughty little boy!
Off you go to Nineveh,
said God one day, Your task
to tell them that
I know about their
wickedness. In forty days
I shall destroy.

So did our Jonah move?
No.
He thought along these lines:

God is loving, he'll forgive,
give a second chance, let live.
Will He really kill?
I don't believe He will!
They'll all think I've
     gone mad,
I *won't* do as He says,
it really is too bad!

So off he went,
but not to Nineveh;
caught a boat for Spain in
Jaffa's port. Can you blame him?

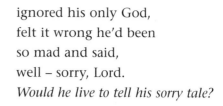

Out at sea,
the storm began.
Full of fear and shaking to a man,
the sailors, terrified, began to pray.
Jonah slept.
Pray, the captain cried.
What can I say, cried Jonah in dismay.
God sent this storm because I ran away.
Throw me overboard, said Jonah,
then the loving Lord, said Jonah,
will soothe the savage seas.
And all the sailors wept.

At last they threw him over in alarm,
watched in wonder as the angry seas
     grew calm.
Every sailor and his captain out of harm
now gave a prayer of thanks to this new God.
But what of Jonah?

The grey waves rose over him,
the wild waves closed over him,
he called to God for help.
Yes, his Lord had followed him,
sent a fish which swallowed him!
Safe inside the whale he wallowed in
     despair.

Alone, afraid and sad,
for three dark days he stayed
inside the murky cavern of the whale.
Jonah thought;
wished he never had

ignored his only God,
felt it wrong he'd been
so mad and said,
well – sorry, Lord.
Would he live to tell his sorry tale?

At last the time was come.
With a wriggle and a shlurp
and a tidal wave of burp
the whale now cast out
Jonah on a beach.
With danger out of reach
he thanked the Lord for sun.

Straight away
he went to Nineveh,
took the message to the people,
and the people, they believed;
changed their ways so utterly
that God did not destroy them
and – can you guess? – Yes!
Jonah felt aggrieved.

Sat down outside the city,
moaned he'd known
what God would do; gave a sigh
half full of anger, half self-pity,
asked God now to leave him there to die.

God said no.
Sent a plant to grow
and shade him from the desert sun,
made him feel much better yet again.
But then
            next day
                  the plant
                        began
                              to die.

I liked that plant,
said Jonah, sad; I'm
sorry that it's gone.
I may seem just a
     moaner, but
I just don't understand.
You are sorry for a plant,
I was sorry for a nation

that I'd given life, said God.
I saw that in their fashion
they had learnt.

And Jonah,
head in hand
on that gold and burning sand
began to think,
began to feel,
began to see.

At last, he said, I think I understand.

Judith Nicholls

Activity

Read the poem about Jonah and paraphrase the story of Jonah from the Bible. What was it Jonah finally understood? Why do you think it took a plant and a worm to teach Jonah this lesson? The poem can be read as a dramatic poem with different pupils taking the various parts.

Searcher

Princess, what are you dreaming,
down among the moist rushes?

Soft pleated linen, beaded bracelets,
purple grapes and Pharaoh's finest wines
await you at the palace –

yet you follow
a wavering baby's cry.

Judith Nicholls

Activity

Read the story of Moses in the bulrushes (Exodus 2.1–10). Who is the searcher in Judith Nicholls's poem? Whose cry does she follow? Why do you think she followed the cry? What did that moment's curiosity lead to? Pupils can draw thought bubbles for the princess, to sum up her thoughts.

Hair 543 ...

Hair 54329635 fell
out today.
God noticed.

Joan Brockelsby

Activity

Read Luke 12.7. Does the writer really mean God sits counting hairs? What meaning does this expression carry? Draw a cartoon to communicate the meaning of this passage.

Dramatic poems

Poems can be read dramatically. The following two poems can be read by more than one voice and the ideas can be followed up afterwards.

Things to think about
(1)   The type of audience. Choose a poem appropriate for the age group and context.

(2)   Go through issues raised by the poem with the pupils, so that they understand what they are saying and can interpret it dramatically when they speak.

(3)   Give pupils time to become familiar with the poem and learn it by heart if possible.

(4)   Choose voices suitable for the parts.

(5)   Copy out the poem in the centre of a large sheet of paper. (Please check your copyright licence.) Pupils can make notes around the edge, noting which parts need emphasizing and how the parts need delivering. Gesture and movement can also be added.

(6)   Practise reading into a tape recorder. Play it back, and work out how the reading can be improved.

(7)   Decide whether you need costumes.

(8)   Write an introduction to your poem which will help the audience understand what it is about.

Resource
Whisked Away: Poems for More Than One Voice
by R Brown (Cambridge University Press, 1993)

One Christmas Eve
For six voices

One snowy Christmas Eve a child opens the door and sees ghostlike figures from the Christmas story. Why have they come? Why do they look so faint and transparent? Is it all a dream?

Child   I opened the door
                 upon a snowy hill.
                 There stood a sheep
                 like a phantom, so still.
                 "Where have you come from,

                 my little sheep,
                 when all of your kind
                 are huddled in sleep?"

Sheep   I have seen stars
                 that from the sky
                 turned into angels,
                 made men cry.
                 I have heard voices
                 that sang of a king,
                 the hills ablaze
                 with the light of their wings.

Child   What is that wavering
                 like a strange ghost,
                 there – a pale man –
                 by the shadowy post?

Shepherd I was a shepherd
                 on that singing night
                 when we were all summoned
                 to a birth of light.
                 Confused, we all were,
                 to leave our sheep,
                 but we had a journey,
                 a promise to keep.

Child   And is that behind you,
                 nodding its head,
                 a ghost of a donkey
                 with silent tread?

Donkey   I was a part
                 of that holy day,

so thankful to munch
the innkeeper's hay;
so shaken, too,
when I heard that cry,
shaken, then stilled
by the mother's sigh.

Sheep I followed on
where the shepherd led,
walking through streets
without any dread ...

Shepherd All of us bathed
in the unnatural light
that haloed the head
of the babe that night.

Star And I shone down
from mysteries afar,
guiding three camels
by the glint of my star,
pulled through the night
on invisible thread
to lead three kings
to an infant's bed.

Camel I was confused
when we came to a king
whose soft-sounding words
had a snakelike sting.
But then, travelling on,
my masters soon found
where to lay presents
on hallowed ground.

Shepherd Animals and angels,
poor shepherds too,
a king in the hay,
a star in the blue,
thus did we stand
and wonder why
God sent this infant
down from on high.

Child Why do you come now,
why to me,
haunting this hillside
by the sea?
Long since those days
have passed us by;
we remember that eve
if we but try;
Bethlehem's gone,
you've strayed so far,
Sheep and Shepherd,
Camel and Star.

All but It's ours to wander
the Child through others' sleep,
to raise our story
from the deep.
Touched by that light
we try to keep
vigil for each child
lost in sleep.

Child But now you are fading –
why do you go?
Fainter than shadows,
colder than snow.
Thank you for coming
this Christmas Eve;
that you were all here
I'll try and believe ...

Empty the night now,
empty the hill;
was there anything there
in the starry chill?

Richard Brown

A creature to sum up Creation
A poem to read around the class

1	Over the whole earth
2	flowers teemed trees stretched shrubs rooted.
1	Over the whole earth
2	lions roared elephants pondered gazelles sped.
1	Over the whole earth
2	mosquitoes buzzed worms burrowed ladybirds settled.
1	In the wide sky
2	eagles gilded doves swarmed swallows dipped.
1	In the vast ocean
2	whales sang sharks prowled salmons leapt.
3	But where was Man Woman Child?
1, 2 & 3	Unmade. There was no Woman, Man, Child yet.
3	The God of Creation said
God	I want a creature to sum up Creation. You animals, you birds, you insects what should Child, Woman, Man be like?

Lion	They should have a roar to make the leaves tremble.
Jaguar	They should have speed to outdistance the wind.
Elephant	They should have strength to shift the mountains.
Monkey	They should have tongues to know how to chatter.
Butterfly	They should have beauty to rival the flowers.
Swallow	They should have wings to give them lightness.
Salmon	They should have gills to swim the great rivers.
Mole	They should have hands to tear the earth.
God	But what should they be like inside themselves?
Gazelle	They should have shyness to know when to hide.
Swan	They should have serenity to know when to drift.
Peacock	They should have vanity to dazzle their thoughts.
Swallow	They should have instinct to guide their journeys.
Tiger	They should have courage to fight their fears.
Tortoise	They should have dreams to fill winter nights.
Lark	They should have song to lift them high.

Dove   They should have hearts
              to fall in love.

God   All these things I can combine.
              But what alone beyond all these
              should I bestow?
All   The spirit, which is your breath.

Richard Brown

Poems as springboards

There are many good non-biblical poems which can be used as springboards into a biblical story or theme. It is important to respect the integrity of the poem and use it as a starting point, not to try to twist it into a biblical poem.

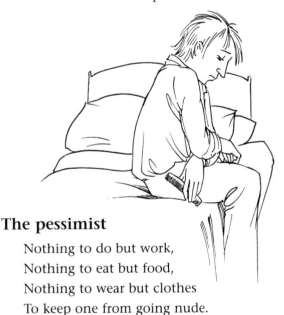

The pessimist

Nothing to do but work,
Nothing to eat but food,
Nothing to wear but clothes
To keep one from going nude.

Nothing to breathe but air,
Quick as a flash 'tis gone;
Nowhere to fall but off,
Nowhere to stand but on.

Nothing to comb but hair,
Nowhere to sleep but in bed,
Nothing to weep but tears,
Nothing to bury but dead.

Nothing to sing but songs,
Ah, well, alas! alack!
Nowhere to go but out,
Nowhere to come but back.

Nothing to see but sights,
Nothing to quench but thirst,
Nothing to have but what we've got;
Thus thro' life we are cursed.

Nothing to strike but a gait;
Everything moves that goes.
Nothing at all but common sense
Can ever withstand these woes.

Ben King

Activity

Talk about being bored in the summer holidays and feeling there is nothing to do. Explain what a pessimist is and read the poem. Pessimists look on the bad side of everything. Everything is seen as boring or bad. A game called "optimist and pessimist" can be played in a circle. Label the pupils alternately optimist and pessimist. The first person, an optimist, makes a positive statement such as "The weather is fine today." The next person has to cap it with a pessimistic statement such as "The forecast said it would rain." This goes on around the group until everyone has had one turn. Pessimists can find nothing for which to say thank you, nothing to rejoice about. In the Bible, Paul talks about rejoicing always and giving thanks for what we have (Philippians 4.4–7). This is the opposite of being pessimistic: it is deliberately looking for things to enjoy, for which you can say thank you to God.

Myself

I have to live with myself, and so
I want to be fit for myself to know.
I want to be able as days go by
Always to look myself straight in the eye.
I don't want to stand with the setting sun
And hate myself for the things I've done.

E A Guest

Activity

Ask the pupils to write a description of a good friend before reading the poem. Do we live up to our expectations of others as expressed in these descriptions? Read the poem. Talk about the way we all do things we regret. We don't always live up to the expectations we have of ourselves.

This can be a springboard for exploring forgiveness and change in stories such as Zacchaeus (Luke 19.1–10).

The meaning of love (an extract)

I love liquorice and I love pop;
I love the smell in the baker's shop.
I love Tennyson, our tabby cat;
I love chips in sizzling fat.
I love roundabouts, dodgems, slides;
I love the seaside – donkey-rides,
Sticks of rock and salty smells.
I love the sound of distant bells
Carried by summer's evening breeze
Over the fields, above the trees,

Tumbling in the trembling air …
But wait a second! Now I find
All this time I've been deaf and blind
To what "love" really means. You see,
The things I've listed here might be
Enjoyable and dear to me;
But love them? No, that's not quite true.

We shouldn't say it,
    though we do.
Love is something
    different:
It's magical, will
    re-invent
Yourself and all the world
    you know;
You don't need me to tell you so.

Vernon Scannell

Activity

After reading the poem together, ask the pupils to select one thing the poet "loves". Ban the word "love" and ask them to rewrite the line without using it, but still conveying what the poet intends. The poet declares that "love" is a much-misused word: we use it to describe our feelings for everything from chips to people. Christians use it to describe God (God is Love: 1 John 4.8). What does the word mean in this context? Paul describes love in detail in 1 Corinthians 13. Using that description, can you write a poem on the biblical concept of love starting with the words "Love is …"?

I don't believe in Human Tales

I don't believe there's such a thing
As nasty little boys.
I think that someone dreams them up;
It's one of the gnome-up's ploys.

I don't believe in super-stores
Where bits of wings and legs
Of harmless little chickens
Are sold in plastic bags.

I'm sure it is just rubbish
That we get turned to stone

If we go near garden ponds
When we're playing out alone.

I'm sure gnome-ups invent these things
To scare us little gnomes
So we'll never leave the forest
Under which we will have our homes.

Brian Patten

Activity

This poem is about belief. The gnome does not believe in superstores or nasty boys. Bring in a small gnome (cheap plaster ones are available from shops). Ask the pupils how they could prove to the gnome that such things existed. This can be a springboard for exploring belief in God. Can such a belief be "proved"? The Bible never sets out to prove the existence of God: it assumes it. If possible, interview Christians about their belief in God.

Thirty poetry activities

All the activities below can be used on biblically based poems but are also applicable to poems in general.

(1) No room!

Divide the class into groups of about six. Give each group a poem on a biblical subject. Explain to the pupils that the editor wants to include biblical poems in a book for pupils their age (or the teacher can specify any age group). Tell them that the editor only has room for three poems out of the six. In groups, they can discuss their poem and make a case for it being included. A vote can be taken after all the poems and arguments have been heard.

(2) Writing letters

Give pupils time to write a letter to a Christian poet asking him or her about their poetry or about the meaning of a particular poem. This can be a creative exercise – the letters are not necessarily for posting!

(3) Pictures from poems

Pupils can draw pictures from poems. Many poems are very visual and create images in the mind. These can be translated into pictures, or pupils can focus on one image and draw that. These can be used to illustrate a poem but should be far more than "drawing a picture": they should try to capture the mood, meaning and images.

(4) Christian poets

Invite a Christian poet into school to read their own poems. Ask them how their beliefs affect their work. What role does the Bible play in their work?

(5) Top ten

Read pupils a number of poems over a period of time, then display them. Ask the pupils to create a "top ten" (or three) of Christian poetry. Pupils should be able to justify their choice.

(6) Read aloud

Give the pupils a poem which they must prepare for reading aloud by one or more voices. Ask them to write directions for the effective delivery of the poem in way that will communicate its meaning. Pupils should have the opportunity to deliver a poem either individually or as part of a group.

(7) Debate

Set up a debate on the issues raised in a poem. For example, is Easter really suitable for children? See the poem on page 94.

(8) Assembly

Pupils can design a series of acts of worship or assemblies each using a poem based on a biblical passage. Add music, Bible readings, prayers, and so on.

(9) Learning by heart

Learn a poem by heart. This allows pupils to concentrate on delivery in oral work.

(10) First impressions, last impressions

Read a poem to the pupils and ask them to write their first impressions. Leave it a week, then read it again and ask them to write their final impressions. How have their impressions changed, if at all?

(11) Poetry swap

Pupils should be allowed to browse through Christian poetry books and select a favourite poem. This can be shared with others, and reasons given for why they like it.

(12) Tapes

Create a tape of a poem so that it can be played to another class or used in an assembly.

(13) Discussion

Read a poem and then divide the class into groups to discuss it. Results of these discussions can be recorded and reported back.

(14) Good points and bad points

After reading a poem, ask pupils to list what they liked about it and what they disliked.

(15) Mime

Pupils can develop mime to go alongside poems.

(16) Dance a poem

Read a poem to the pupils and ask them to interpret it in dance. Words reflecting movement in the poem can be the basis for dance. A suitable poem would be "The World" by W Brighty Rands from *Whispering in God's Ear* compiled by A MacDonald (Lion).

(17) Music

Select pieces of music to go with a poem. This can be played beforehand or the poem can be read over the top of it. Pupils can also pick up the rhythm and sounds within poetry to develop in music.

(18) Sound effects

Sound effects can be added to a poem. Pupils can write down appropriate sounds to communicate the mood of a poem.

(19) Stills

Freeze a moment from a poem to draw as a still from a film or arrange people as a still from the poem and take a photograph.

(20) Tableaux

Pupils can create a tableau on the subject of the poem. The tableau can come alive at a particular moment and the pupils can improvise what the characters might have said. See page 99, *Story and Drama*.

(21) Play scripts

Pupils can translate narrative poems into a play or a play script.

(22) Dramatic reading

Poems can be read dramatically, in costume if desired.

(23) Storyboard

What is the story of the poem? Can you make a storyboard of it? See page 110, *Story and Drama*. The poem on Jonah, page 94, would be a good subject for this.

(24) Appreciation and criticism

Give various groups different poems but on the same biblical subject. Christmas poems are easiest to find. Each group can prepare a reading and an appreciation and criticism for other groups. Pupils can also list similarities and differences.

(25) Change poetry to prose

Ask pupils to tell the story behind a narrative poem. Compare this with the poem. Which is more effective?

(26) Interviews

If you could interview the main character in a poem, what would you ask them? Write down two questions you would like to ask.

(27) Brainstorming

Using large sheets of paper, brainstorm all the emotions and reactions which occur in the poem. These can be classified into positive and negative reactions, and the reasons behind these reactions discussed.

(28) Mental images

Ask the pupils to listen to a poem with their eyes closed, trying to concentrate on the mental picture it builds up. After the poem is finished, ask pupils to share mental pictures. The poem, "John, John the Baptist" page 93 would be good for this activity.

(29) Using visitors

Invite a Christian into school and ask how they use poetry as part of worship, or to share poems which are meaningful to them as a Christian.

(30) Matching

Match poems on a biblical subject to the original story. How well has the poet expressed the meaning and significance of the story?

DETAILED ACTIVITIES

Senses poems

Jeremiah in the well: Jeremiah 38.1–13
The burning bush: Exodus 3.1–12
Mary Magdalene sees Jesus: Mark 16.9–11; John 20.11–18

Description of the activity

This technique involves the pupils listening to a story
and then describing it with reference to all the senses:
what could be felt, smelt, tasted, seen and heard. The
poems can be written from the point of view of one
character in the story: what *they* sensed.

The poem should be five lines in length, each line
dealing with a different sense. The pupils can add a sixth
line if they wish, exploring what the character felt
emotionally. Symbols for the different senses can be
placed at the beginning of each line. The symbols can be
photocopied and given to the pupils. They can cut these
out and paste them at the beginning of the relevant lines.
The lines can be in any order. For some stories only a few
senses would be used. Pupils can draw a heart to
symbolize what the character was feeling emotionally.

Examples

From Rainey Endowed School, Magherafelt, Northern Ireland.

Mary

I can see him dying on the cross,
I can hear the low moaning as his life slowly disappears.
I can smell the bitter perfume they poured over his body.
I can taste the tears running down my cheeks into my mouth,
I can feel his pain

Thomas Scott, Year 3

The burning bush

A burning bush that didn't burn,
A shepherd on a lonely hill,
He smelt the burning,
He saw the bush,
He heard the calling,
Felt the presence of the Lord,
Tasted the love of God,
As he touched the holy ground.

Marlene Boyd, Year 3

Mary outside the tomb (extract)

She cradled her loss and pain outside where he'd lain,
With the mysterious tomb, so cold and untold,
She was there with her withering memories alone.
She gazed once again into the weary emptiness.

Tracey Kane, Year 3

Biblical application

This technique can be applied to a large number of stories. Some stories will contain elements that will emphasize one sense more than others. In the case of the burning bush, the pupils could explore what all of Moses' senses were recording and how he felt. The emphasis in the story of Mary Magdalene would be different, less on touch, and more on sight and sound. In the case of Jeremiah there might be more emphasis on touch. Once the pupils are familiar with the technique they can use it freely just incorporating a few senses.

Random poems

The creation: Genesis 1.1—2.25
Crossing the red sea: Exodus 13.17—14.31
The coming of the Holy Spirit: Acts 2.1–13

Description of the activity

After listening to a story, pupils make lists of

- nouns from the story or associated with it;
- verbs to describe the action of the story;
- as many adjectives as possible to describe the nouns;
- adverbs to describe the verbs.

All the nouns are written on separate pieces of paper and are cut up and put in paper bags or boxes. This is repeated with verbs, adjectives, and adverbs. Pupils take turns at selecting pairs of words – adverbs and verbs, adjectives and nouns. If they select a pair they like, they are written up on a large sheet of paper. The words are then returned to the bag, stirred, and someone else chooses.

The result should be lots of pairs of words which can be used in two ways: some pupils may choose to select pairs of words to use in longer poems, others may create short poems using only pairs of random words as in the examples.

NOTE: There are computer programs which will produce random poetry using this technique.

Pupils can make their own random selector using strips of paper and four slots in a piece of cardboard. The strips of paper are pulled independently to produce random selections. Younger pupils can use just nouns and adjectives.

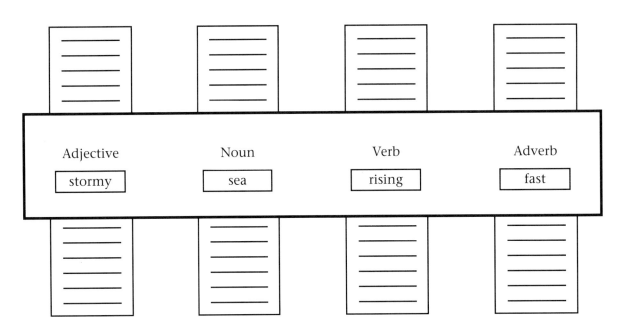

Examples of nouns and adjectives selected from the story of the crossing of the Red Sea.

NOUNS	ADJECTIVES
sea	stormy
wind	howling
chariots	threatening
wheels	spinning

Examples of random selection from those words:

spinning wind

howling water

threatening wheels

These words can then be incorporated into a poem about the crossing of the Red Sea.

Examples

Terrified chariots
Howling birds
Wild water
Gusty fear
Worried Israelites
Frantically scared
Threatening wind
Crawling reluctantly
Slowly believing
Striding safely
The Israelites left.

Rebekah Walker, Year 7, George Spencer School, Stapleford

Rejoicing happily
Evil King, seeking revenge
Faithful Israelites, praying peacefully
Enormous camp fire
Armed Egyptians approaching noisily
Gleaming chariots
Army hoping to cross amazingly
Bright Moses arguing loudly
Brilliant victory

Paul Smith, Year 6, Robert Shaw Primary School, Nottingham

Biblical application

This can be used on many stories from the Bible but the teacher needs to choose stories where there is lots of action and reaction in order to supply an adequate number of words. Pupils can listen to the story of the crossing of the Red Sea, the creation or the coming of the Holy Spirit and use the technique described above. As the random words are selected pupils should discuss whether that description is suitable for the story, does it communicate the meaning? Often unusual combinations of words spark trains of thought and discussion.

Alliteration

Creation: Genesis 1.1—2.25
Peter walks on water: Matthew 14.22–32
The transfiguration: Matthew 17.1–13; Mark 9.2–13; Luke 9.28–36

Description of the activity

Alliteration is when words with matching initial sounds are used, such as forest and ferny, one and water. Pupils can be introduced to this technique by using tongue twisters such as "Peter Piper picked a piece of pickled pepper." Pupils can write their own tongue twisters for practice using a dictionary.

This is a well-known technique with a long history. Anglo-Saxon poetry uses alliteration, as do many of the old miracle plays. Alliteration is best used sparingly, as in "The Listeners" by Walter De La Mare.

> "Is there anybody there?" said the Traveller,
> Knocking on the moonlit door;
> And his horse in the silence champed the grasses
> Of the *forest's ferny floor:*

From the York miracle plays
> "Thou maker that most is of might,
> To thy mercy I now make my moan."

An example

God made the —

Giant Giraffes
Slithering Snakes
Purple Parrots
Black Bat
Treacle Trees
Beautiful Butterfly
Lovely Ladybird
Squabbling Squirrels
Friendly Frog
Massive Mountains
Tall Trees

And saw that it was good.

Rebecca McConnon, Laura Marinelli, Geoffrey Yeomans, Jennifer Oswin, Rebecca Marshall, and Wendy Wardle, aged 8–9 years, Albany County Primary School, Stapleford

Biblical application

The technique can be applied to many stories of the Bible. Pupils should locate key words in the story, words which cover both content and meaning, and create alliterative descriptions for them. For example, in the story of the Good Samaritan alliterative descriptions can be created for each of the main characters and then placed in order, to tell the story.

Tired traveller
Rough road
Threatening thieves
Broken body
Proud priests
Hard hearts
Helping hand.

The same method can be used for the transfiguration and Peter on the water, and the resulting pairs of words can be incorporated into longer poems or the pairs can be put together to form a poem as above.

The story of creation can be expressed using alliteration. Divide the pupils into a number of groups to cover different parts of the creation story. Pupils can then select various key words and events from their part of the story. Alliterative words can be selected to go with these. For a creation poem, each verse can have its own pattern and structure. Pupils do not have to work to a common scheme. The finished verses can be put together when completed.

List poems

Love: Song of Songs 8.6–7
Anger: Ephesians 4.26
Fear: Psalm 46.1–2
Worry: Matthew 6.25; Proverbs 12.25
Envy and Jealousy: Proverbs 27.4; Song of Songs 8.6–7
Pride: Proverbs 16.18
Deceit: Proverbs 20.17
Selfishness: Proverbs 21.13
Generosity: Proverbs 22.8
Evil speech: Proverbs 12.18
Wealth: Ecclesiastes 5.10–12
Peace: Proverbs 14.30
Kind words: Proverbs 15.4

Description of the Activity

List poems, at their most simple level, are easy to write. They can be lists which describe a quality or emotion "Peace is ..." "Love is ...". They can also be interpretative as well as descriptive. After discussing and researching a particular subject, pupils can include some of the insights gained in their list poem.

Examples

These were all written by Year 9 pupils from Newcastle-under-Lyme School.

Love
Is
A light for the future
A blazing fire forever
A partnership shared by two
A commitment made by both
For love is strong as death
And passion is as cruel as the grave

Hilary Latham

Pride
Is
Dogmatic.
Never gives in
Just to be
Awkward
Lindsay Lowe

Wealth
Is
Fortune
Or a poor man
Surrounded
By
Friends
Miranda Harris

Peace
Is
A tranquil mind
A silent room
Still waters
Calmness
Relaxation
Jenna Culley

Deceit
Is
Sweet at first
Afterwards
You'll feel guilty
Discovered
Regretful
It Leads to a
Mouth
Full
Of
Grit...
Lizzie Gordon

Biblical application

The list poem format can be used to explore various qualities such as Love, Joy, Envy. Biblical quotations on some of these subjects are listed. Give each pupil a quotation from the list above. The quotation, or part of it, can be used as the title of the poem. The pupils start their poem "Love is ...," "Hatred is ...," "Envy is ...," and write a short poem which reflects the Bible's perspective on that particular feeling or quality, as well as the pupils' own thinking about it. This technique helps pupils look at a perspective on an emotion other than their own or the one current in society. Often the biblical perspective will be new to pupils and time will be needed to discuss this way of looking at things.

Sound poems

The fall of Jericho: Joshua 5.13—6.27
The still small voice: 1 Kings 19.1–18
Jesus and the money-changers: Matthew 21.12–17; Mark 11.15–17; Luke 19.45–48

Description of the activity

This technique is like watching the television with the volume up and the contrast so dark that you cannot see the picture. You cannot see what is going on, you can only hear the sounds

The pupils read a story and write down all the sounds that might have been going on. The description of these sounds is then used to retell the story so that the reader of the poem can imagine from the sounds what is happening.

An example

Jericho

Grit crunches,
Metal swords tingle and crash.
The wind blowing like the sea.
The rain like seeds falling.
Nothing but people marching.

The sound of people marching,
Trumpets loud as thunder,
Shouting hard as an earthquake.
A hurricane of bricks and people.

Sukhmeet Mann, Matthew Mee, and Jamie Hallam, Year 4, Albany County Primary School, Stapleford

Biblical application

This activity works best on stories with a range of noises such as those of Jericho, the entry into Jerusalem (Palm Sunday), Jesus and the money-changers, or Elijah and the still small voice. Pupils read the story and list the various sounds. They decide which are the most important sounds to convey the message of the story.

Ask them to describe the sounds by listing what the sound is like. For example, the rain may sound like seeds falling. The images and sounds can then be incorporated into a poem (it can be any form) in a way that will retell the story and catch its meaning. They need to make sure they include the sounds they listed as most significant.

If pupils have not used this technique before, give them several examples of sound poems.

Cinquain

God's promise to Abraham: Genesis 12.2; 15.1–21; 17.7,8; 17.15–19; 18.1–15
Esau sells his birthright: Genesis 25.27–34
The woman with a haemorrhage: Matthew 9.20–22; Mark 5.25–34; Luke 8.43–48

Description of the activity

The cinquain, like the haiku, is a syllable-counting poem. It was invented by an American, Adelaide Crapsey. The form has five lines containing a total of 22 syllables with a syllable pattern of 2, 4, 6, 8, 2.

The first and last lines are sometimes difficult to form. If this is so, the poem can be written from the middle – the beginning and end being added later. The end should have some impact and, as with the Haiku, the emphasis should be on meaning.

Young children can try a variation on the cinquain which involves using a similar pattern, but counting words rather than syllables. The first line has one word, the second, two words, the third three words the fourth, four and the last line has one word. With this format, the first word should be the title and the last word should have particular impact.

Read several examples of cinquains to the pupils to give them practice at counting the syllables. Neutral examples are best for this; see the two following examples.

Cinquains
Are easier
If you count up feelings
Then photograph the intended
Impact

Chris Guest

Cinquain:
A short verse form
Of counted syllables ...
And first devised by Adelaide
Crapsey.

Gerard Benson

Examples

Counting syllables
Noah
> Relief
> Touching homeland,
> The rivers and mountains.
> Beautiful, delighted rainbow,
> Safety.

Martyn Gilmour, Year 4, Lowe's Wong Junior School, Southwell

Counting words
The woman with a haemorrhage
> Bleeding,
> So silently.
> Touching soft wool
> Desperate to be healed.
> Saved.

Robert Cooling, Year 9, George Spencer School, Stapleford

Biblical application
As this form emphasizes meaning, it can be used to explore any story. The pupils should listen to the story, and decide on one moment to explore using a cinquain, attempting not only to capture a picture of the moment, but also to sum up its meaning or the feelings involved.

Metaphors and similes

The "I am" sayings: John 6.35; 8.12; 9.5; 10.9; 10.11; 11.25, 14.6; 15.1; 15.5
Elijah on Mount Carmel: 1 Kings 18.16–46
Jonah: The Book of Jonah

Description of the activity

A simile likens one object to another, a metaphor says one object *is* another.

"The sun was a ball of fire" is a metaphor but "She went as white as a sheet" is a simile. Similes tend to use "as" or "like". Both forms try to convey meaning by the way they describe one thing by using something else.

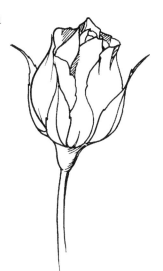

>   My love is like a red, red rose
>   That's newly sprung in June …
>
>   Robert Burns

Pupils can practise similes and metaphors by completing sentences. Give them a number of lines where they have to create the simile or metaphor.

>   The night fell like a …

>   The moon is a …

Pupils can be given a range of objects for which they can create metaphors and similes. The metaphor game can also be used to give pupils experience of using metaphors. For this game, pupils take a character and decide what they would "be" using various categories (such as colour, flower, vegetable or fruit, weather). Pupils choose what they think would best sum up a character's personality.

Goliath

> If he were a tree he would be a giant oak.
> If he were a flower he would be a thistle,
> If he were a vegetable he would be a swede.
> If he were a colour he would be purple.
> If he were weather he would be a thunderstorm.

An example

Mary

> If she were a flower she would be a snowdrop.
> If she were weather she would be sunny.
> If she were a bird she would be a dove.
> If she were a fruit she would be a sweet apple.
> If she were an animal she would be a tiny mouse.

Rachael Walker, Year 4, Fairfield Primary School, Stapleford

Biblical application

The Bible itself uses simile and metaphor in its poetry. Pupils can explore some of the poems of the Bible for their similes and metaphors (Psalm 18.2, 30, 33; Job 38.14) and explore what the writer was trying to communicate. Jesus uses metaphor of himself in the "I am" sayings. Again, pupils can explore the meanings of these.

The metaphor game can be used to explore various biblical characters such as Jonah and Elijah.

The song of...

The good Samaritan: Luke 10.25–37
The lost coin: Luke 15.8–10
The stilling of the storm: Matthew 8.23–27

Description of the activity
In this technique an object speaks and its speech forms the poem. This is a technique with a long history: the Saxon poem "The Dream of the Rood" is the cross of Jesus telling its own story, the modern poem "The History of the Flood" by John Heath Stubbs has the nails of the ark telling the story of Noah.

The pupils listen to a story and choose an object from within it. The object can comment, ask questions, tell the story, and bring out the meaning.

Examples
The song of the fishing boat

> Just another trip across the lake.
> My life has been spent as a fishing boat.
> I always wanted to be a big ship.
> A storm comes upon the lake.
> I feel scared, cold and damp.
> I cannot fight this storm,
> Jesus can.
> He wakes up and says "Quiet! be still"
> And I am safe.

Shane Bridges, Year 4, Bishop John Robinson School, Thamesmead

The song of the cross

Still and gentle,
Waving my leaves in the breeze
And crash I was cut down.
My dreams faded away.
Gone forever.
I was cut into beams of wood.
I felt wasted, useless.
I was nailed to the ground
A man was nailed to me.
I was facing up to heaven,
I felt I was special, magnificent, great.
I felt so good, as if I was God.

Natasha Goodman, Year 4, Bishop John Robinson School, Thamesmead

Biblical application

This technique can be used on virtually any biblical story. It could be the Song of the
Palm for Palm Sunday, or the Song of the Coin in the story of the Lost Coin. In the case
of the Good Samaritan, pupils could choose to be the road, the rocks – whatever they
think would be a good subject to tell the story and bring out its meaning. The pupils
then write a poem (it can be in any form) which tells the story from the object's point of
view and makes comments about what it is happening.

Haiku

Joseph the slave: Genesis 39.1—40.23
Paul escapes: Acts 9.19–31
The man with the withered hand: Matthew 12.9–14

Description of the activity

Both Haiku and Cinquains involve the pupils in counting syllables. Practice in this may
need to be given first. Syllables can be equated with beats, and pupils practise tapping the
syllables of different words and phrases with percussion instruments.

A Haiku is a short Japanese form of poetry. An English form of the Haiku has three
lines. The first line has five syllables, the second, seven, the third, five. It is not an easy
form to use but the basic pattern can be a guide rather than a rigid structure. If a pupil
produces a good poem that has a syllable short or a syllable too many it does not matter.

One way of structuring a Haiku is to see it as a statement followed by a comment; or the lines can be statement followed by image and comment. The thought should be uppermost: the syllables can be adjusted later. Pupils should be given neutral examples on which to practise.

Haiku are icebergs:
Three lines floating on the page,
The rest unwritten

Chris Webster

Poem in three lines:
Five syllables, then seven,
Five again; no rhyme.

Eric Finney

It may seem very restrictive, using only seventeen syllables in a set pattern. This restriction, however, can prove liberating: it makes pupils search for words, rather than writing the obvious. Pupils write first and adjust the syllables later. I have adjusted this poem by a Year 7 pupil from Bishop Ramsey Church of England School, Hillingdon.

The man with the withered hand
A withered hand all crinkled up.
Like paper in a bin.
Then suddenly it blossomed out.

adjusted:

A withered hand. (4)
Crinkled paper in a bin, (7)
Suddenly blossomed. (5)

Biblical application

These techniques are particularly useful in exploring biblical subjects as the emphasis is on catching the significance of a particular moment. The pupils listen to or read the story of Joseph as a slave, Paul escaping, or the man being healed. When they have heard the story ask them to take a photograph in their "mind's eye" of a particular moment, and to jot down in a rough notebook a description of that scene. The Haiku can then be written about that particular moment of the story, capturing its essence and meaning.

Questions

Where were you?: Job 38.4—40.1
Blind Bartimaeus: Mark 10.46–52
Abraham and Isaac: Genesis 22.1–19 (older pupils)

Description of the activity

Single questions can form the starting point of poems. "Who am I?" "What child is this?" "Why me?" The poem consists of the pupil's answers to that question.

A second form of this activity is where there is a question posed by a character in a story, and the poem is an extended answer to that question written by the pupil in role.

Examples

A pupil answers

Who am I?

I am my mind, my thoughts,
my ideas.
I am my trust, my beliefs, my hope.
I am my strengths and weaknesses,
my understanding
I am one who loves, one who can be loved,
one who finds these things vital.
I am part of the people around me
I am one small piece of a jigsaw
But most importantly I am myself —
I am one individual.

Gabi Barker-Boland, Year 9, Peers School, Oxford

A character (Bartimaeus) answers
Jesus: "What do you want me to do for you?"
Bartimaeus: "I want to see again."

I want to see
The people who gave me money,
Myself in a mirror,
Jesus.

I want to see
My village and home,
Food and clothes,
The sun.

Matthew Mee and Sukhmeet Mann, Year 4, Albany County Primary School,
Stapleford

Biblical application

Questions form the basis of many biblical poems: "Where were you when I laid the
foundations of the earth?" is the basis of a long poem from the Book of Job which is full
of repeated questions. Pupils can take some of the questions and develop their own
poems from them which explore the significance of the passage. Abraham could ask
"Why Isaac? Why my only son?"

Free verse

Love: 1 Corinthians 13
Ruth and Naomi: Ruth 1.16–17
Peter calls Jesus "the Christ": Luke 9.18–20

Description of the activity

Free verse has no regular rhyme and rhythm: its effect is created by the position of line breaks. Alliteration can be used (see page 110), and words within a line can rhyme. Free verse has its own irregular rhythm. The arrangement of the lines makes the reader think and read the words in a particular way, which helps bring out the meaning. An example of a biblical passage written as free verse can be seen on page 87–8.

Neither the layout nor the construction are random. Pupils should spend time thinking about the best way to lay out a poem to bring out the meaning. One way of starting pupils on this exercise is to give them pieces of prose which can be arranged as free verse. Photocopy a short amount of prose from the Good News Bible and give it to the pupils, who should be grouped in pairs. Ask them to read the prose and write two sentences in their books to sum up its meaning. Give each pair a glue stick, a piece of paper and a pair of scissors. Tell them they are allowed to discard words from the piece of prose which they consider to be unimportant, and they can add a few words to highlight the meaning of the text, providing they stay true to its significance. Some pupils may create their poem without adding or removing anything.

An example

But Ruth replied, "Don't urge me to leave you or to turn back from you. Where you go I will go, and where you stay I will stay. Your people will be my people and your God my God. Where you die I will die, and there will I be buried" (NIV Ruth 1.16,17)

Ruth

Don't urge me
to leave you,
or to turn back.

Where you go,
I will go.

Where you stay,
I will stay.

Your people,
My people.

Your God,
My God.

Where you die,
I die,
And there I will be buried.

Ashley Wilson, Richard Fawcett, and Russel Down, Year 5, Albany County Primary School, Stapleford

Biblical application

Free verse is suitable for many stories of the Bible. Its pauses, unusual line lengths, and irregular rhythm help bring the meaning uppermost. For example, important words can be highlighted by standing on their own. Pupils can "cut and paste" biblical passages such as 1 Corinthians 13 or Peter calling Jesus the Christ, using the "cut and paste" facility of the computer. It must be stressed that this is only a first step towards pupils writing their own free verse on a biblical subject. Once they have mastered creating free verse from prose, pupils can go on to write their own free verse.

NOTE: A version of 1 Corinthians 13 arrranged as free verse can be found on page 87–8.

Kennings

Abraham leaves home: Genesis 11.31; 12.1–9
David: 1 Samuel 16.1–23; 17.1–58; 18.1–16
John the Baptist: Matthew 3.1–12; 14.1–12

Description of the activity

This technique involves an object, person or event being indicated by a description rather than being directly named. The sea might be the "whale-road", a ship a "horse of the sea", a train an "iron horse", and whisky "fire-water". This technique was used by the Vikings and aboriginal Americans.

Before using this technique to explore the Bible, give pupils a number of objects and ask them to create kennings for them. This can be done by giving them a pack of "Post It" notes and asking them to write kennings for particular objects on the "notes". The "Post It" notes can then be stuck on the relevant objects around the room.

Pencil = paper-eater   computer disk = fact-spinner

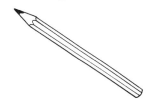
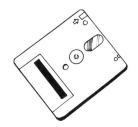

Examples
David

> Sheep-lover
> Harp-player
> Giant-killer
> Mini army.

Wendy Wardle, Rebecca Marshall, and Jennifer Oswin, Year 4, Albany Junior School, Stapleford

Daniel

> Lion tamer
> Miracle man
> Scared of nothing
> Praying man
> Friend of God
> Firm stander.

Alison Birch, Laura Colley, Chris Hart, Andrew Ditch, Gary Cox, and Samantha Earp, Year 6, St Peter's Church of England School, Cannock

Biblical application

This technique can be used to examine people's characters or the role played by certain objects, places or events in Bible stories. Various kennings can be devised to describe Jesus: "Heart-healer", "Cross-bearer". Pupils should study a story such as the life of David. They should select significant episodes, people, places or objects in those stories using a number of kennings. The same can be done for the life of John the Baptist, Abraham, or any other biblical character.

The separate kennings can be put together to form a poem, or they can form part of longer lines, as in "The word-weaver sang to the troubled king" (David playing the harp to King Saul).

Time, person, place, and weather

The Christmas story: Matthew 1.18–25; 2.1–12; Luke 2.1–20
The ten lepers: Luke 17.11–19
Joseph as a boy: Genesis 37.1–36

Description of the activity

This activity is an adaptation of a technique first devised by Russell Hoban. Pupils listen to a story and then decide on four co-ordinates.

- They choose a time (be specific).
- Pupils choose a person from the story.
- They select a place from the story.
- They decide what the weather is like.

This narrows pupils down to a precise moment and a particular situation which can give them a firm starting-point for poetry or prose. Finished sets of co-ordinates for the Christmas story might be:

Time: 5.30 a.m.
Person: A shepherd
Place: On a hillside
Weather: Dry and cold

Time: 12.30 p.m.
Person: Mary
Place: Street
Weather: Spitting with hail and cold

An example
From the Christmas Story
The light on his face

> I felt cold and tired.
> How must Joseph feel,
> all this pressure on him?
> But he's as strong as a bull.
> Suddenly I felt all faint,
> my eyes began to dim,
> I felt like shouting, "Why me?"
> We knocked on a door,
> The pain began.
> A lady answered,
> Joseph explained.
> She said, "Poor lamb,"
> So we had the stable.
> I felt some relief.
> He was born at one
> with light on his face.

Alice Chandler, Year 4, St Paul's Church of England School, Hereford

Biblical application

This technique can be used on wide range of stories, from sagas such as the Joseph story to miracles such as the story of the ten lepers. There needs to be a choice of location and characters, but that applies in the majority of stories. The nature of the activity channels pupils into exploring part of the story in depth rather than ranging over a large amount of material, though they will need to know the complete story.

The Christmas story is an ideal subject. After reading this story ask the pupils to write down any time, day or night. They need to be precise about the time, for example 5.30 a.m. Pupils then choose a character: a wise man, Mary, Joseph. Bearing in mind who they are, they choose a place compatible with the story: Bethlehem, a hillside, a desert. They then decide what the weather is like. They need to look at their previous choices: if they are in the desert, it probably isn't snowing!

Bearing in mind this situation, what would the character be feeling and thinking? Is it after the birth of Jesus, or before?

Pupils can explore the person's feelings in poetry or prose. Across a class, there can be a range of poems exploring various characters. Pupils can write their poem in the centre of a page, and in the corners put drawings to indicate the time, weather, and so on.

Mirror poems

Leah: Genesis 29.15–30
Saul: Samuel 18.1—19.24
Judas: Matthew 26.14–16; Mark 14.10–11; Luke 22.1–6

Description of the activity

This technique involves a character from the story looking in a reflective surface such as metal or water which acts as a "mirror". Start the activity by giving the pupils mirror card or a number of reflective items such as foil or spoons. Ask the pupils to look into their "mirror" and describe in note form all that it reflects. This can be fairly factual: eye colour, hair.

With younger pupils teachers can talk about magic mirrors in stories such as "The Snow Queen" and "Snow White".

If a scientist invented a magic mirror which could reflect not only a person's outside but also their feelings and thoughts, would it sell?

Poems can be written about characters who peer into mirrors, or other reflective surfaces, and the "mirror" reflects back their thoughts and feelings as well as their outside appearance. Pupils can start by making rough notes on what the mirror would reflect of the inside and outside of the character and work these into a poem.

Mirror, mirror on the wall
Who is the fairest of
them all?

An example

Jonah

When Jonah looked in the mirror
He saw a wet man,
A man covered in seaweed,
A man in a whale.

When Jonah looked in the mirror
He saw a frightened man,
A man who disobeyed his God,
A man who was ashamed.

When Jonah looked in the mirror
He saw a bad man,
A man who looked sorry for himself,
A man who was frightened.

Gemma Dexter, Year 6, St John's Church of England School, Stapleford

Biblical application

This can be used in most biblical stories. All that is needed is a reflective surface, such as a piece of armour, a metal pot, or a pool of water. In the case of Leah, if she had looked into her mirror what would she have seen? Pupils should describe not only how they think she looked but also her thoughts and feelings. If Judas had stared into a pool, what would he have seen? What would Saul have seen if he had caught sight of himself in a piece of armour and it mirrored what he was like on the inside?

Shape poems

John the Baptist: Matthew 3.1–12; Mark 1.1–18; Luke 3.1–18; John 1.19–28
The empty tomb: Matthew 28.1–7; Mark 16.1–10; Luke 24.1–12; John 20.1–10
Light of the world: John 8.12

Description of the activity
In this activity, the pattern or shape the poem makes reflects the subject of the poem. The poem can either be written within a shape or the words can form a particular pattern. Pupils need to hear the story several times. Drama can also be used to stimulate ideas.

Examples
Crossing the Red Sea

Mark Timmins, age 11, Robert Shaw Primary School, Aspley, Nottingham

The next two examples are not shape poems as such but an adaption of the technique.

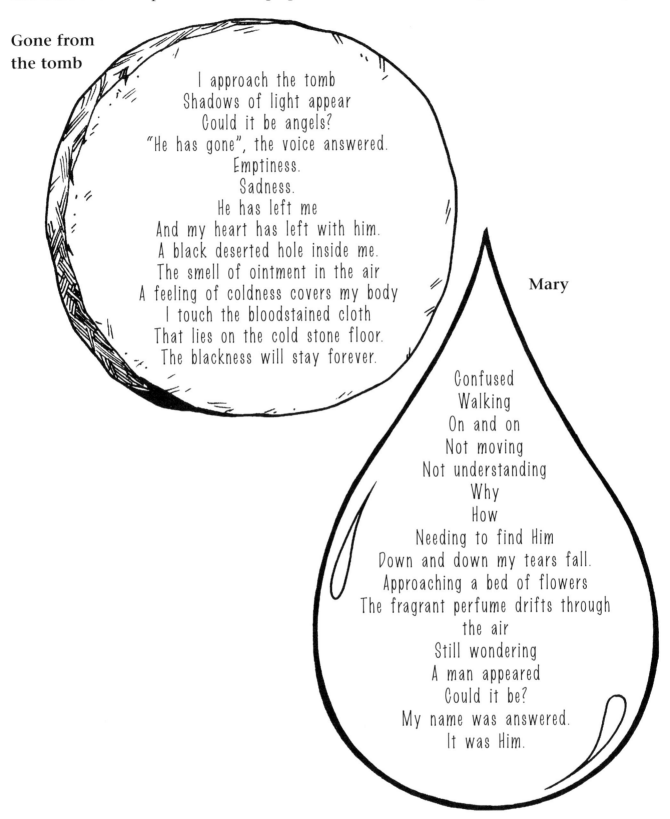

Gone from the tomb

I approach the tomb
Shadows of light appear
Could it be angels?
"He has gone", the voice answered.
Emptiness.
Sadness.
He has left me
And my heart has left with him.
A black deserted hole inside me.
The smell of ointment in the air
A feeling of coldness covers my body
I touch the bloodstained cloth
That lies on the cold stone floor.
The blackness will stay forever.

Mary

Confused
Walking
On and on
Not moving
Not understanding
Why
How
Needing to find Him
Down and down my tears fall.
Approaching a bed of flowers
The fragrant perfume drifts through
the air
Still wondering
A man appeared
Could it be?
My name was answered.
It was Him.

Emily Rose Blades, Year 5, Lantern Lane Primary School, East Leake, Loughborough.

Biblical application

Many biblical stories can be explored using this technique. Poems can be written in the shape of an object or animal from the story. The subject matter of the poem would be the biblical story, from which the object is taken. It is important, therefore, that pupils choose an object which they feel is significant in the story. Pupils should be able to justify their choice and should have time to discuss it. For the story of Mary Magdalene a round stone shape could be used or a tear drop. For the "Light of the world" pupils can write within a candle flame shape, or the words can radiate from a central "flame". Words can be written as waves of water for John the Baptist. Some pupils find the shape too restricting, as Emily did. In such cases the shape can become a very loose framework where it acts as a background rather than a structure which determines the shape of the poem.

STORY INDEX

The initials used below refer to the volume of Toolkit in which the story concerned occurs; *WP Writing and Poetry, SD Story and Drama, AM Art and Music.*